PROPERTY OF TRANS UNION

INVESTING IN INFORMATION TECHNOLOGY

A Decision-Making Guide for Business and Technology Managers

BILL BYSINGER

KEN KNIGHT

VAN NOSTRAND REINHOLD
I(T)P™ A Division of International Thomson Publishing Inc.

New York • Albany • Bonn • Boston • Detroit • London • Madrid • Melbourne
Mexico City • Paris • San Francisco • Singapore • Tokyo • Toronto

Copyright © 1996 by Van Nostrand Reinhold

All rights reserved. No part of this work covered by the copyright hereon may be reproduced or used in any form or by any means—graphic, electronic, or mechanical, including photocopying, recording, taping, or information storage and retrieval systems—without the written permission of the publisher.

I(T)P ™ Van Nostrand Reinhold is an International Thomson Publishing Company. ITP logo is a trademark under license.

Printed in the United States of America.

Van Nostrand Reinhold
115 Fifth Avenue
New York, NY 10003

International Thomson Publishing Germany
Königswinterer Str. 418
53227 Bonn
Germany

International Thomson Publishing
Berkshire House, 168-173
High Holborn
London WC1V 7AA
England

International Thomson Publishing Asia
221 Henderson Building #05-10
Singapore 0315

Thomas Nelson Australia
102 Dodds Street
South Melbourne 3205
Victoria, Australia

International Thomson Publishing Japan
Kyowa Building, 3F
2-2-1 Hirakawacho
Chiyoda-Ku, Tokyo 102
Japan

Nelson Canada
1120 Birchmount Road
Scarborough, Ontario
M1K 5G4, Canada

1 2 3 4 5 6 7 8 9 0 QEBFF 02 01 00 99 98 97 96

Library of Congress Cataloging-in-Publication Data

Bysinger, Bill
   Investing in information technology : a decision making guide for business and technology managers / Bill Bysinger and Ken Knight.
     p. cm.
   Includes index.
   ISBN 0-442-02337-5
   1. Information technology--Decision making. 2. Capital investments--Decision making. I. Knight, Kenneth. II. Title.
HD30.2.B95 1996   96-28507
658.4'038--dc20   CIP

Project Management: Judith Steinbaum
Production: Jo-Ann Campbell • Production: mle design • 562 Milford Point Rd., Milford, CT 06460

This book is dedicated to:

—God, our Father, for giving us the wisdom and guidance to write this book,

—our wives, Sandra and Ann, and our families who encourage us and persevered through the process,

—our business and professional associates who provided the experiences and opportunities on which this book is based.

—and a very special *Thanks* to all the many, many others who helped us in the process of writing this book.

Contents

Prologue	Surviving the Technology Process Shift	vii
Prologue	Surviving the Business Process Shift from the Business Manager's Viewpoint *by Ken Knight*	xi
Prologue	Surviving the Business Process Shift from the Information System Manager's Viewpoint *by Bill Bysinger*	xvi
CHAPTER 1	A Different Agenda: What Does the Business Manager Need to Know? *by Ken Knight*	1
CHAPTER 2	A Different Agenda: Discovering Customers *by Bill Bysinger*	11
CHAPTER 3	Folklore and Fairy Tale: The Advantage from Technology *by Ken Knight*	25
CHAPTER 4	The On Time Project—It Can Be Done *by Bill Bysinger*	45
CHAPTER 5	Business Process Analysis—It Is Not Black Magic *by Ken Knight*	57
CHAPTER 6	The Challenge: Communicating in Business Terms *by Bill Bysinger*	73

CHAPTER 7	How to Implement Technology: Managing for Continual Improvement *by Ken Knight*	83
CHAPTER 8	MIS Process Methodology: "Intrapreneuring" *by Bill Bysinger*	105
CHAPTER 9	Technical Value: Measuring Return on Investment *by Ken Knight*	117
CHAPTER 10	Technology Investment Management: Showing Return *by Bill Bysinger*	147
CHAPTER 11	Innovation to Leverage Technology *by Ken Knight*	161
CHAPTER 12	Products and Measurement: The IS Manager and the Art of Selling *by Bill Bysinger*	173
CHAPTER 13	Creating Heroes: Managing the Technology-Empowered Organization *by Ken Knight*	185
CHAPTER 14	Creating Heroes: Allies in Business *by Bill Bysinger*	201
CHAPTER 15	Making It Simple: Integrating Business Management with Technology *by Bill Bysinger and Ken Knight*	211
	Index	217

PROLOGUE

Surviving the Technology Process Shift

A powerful force is driving businesses toward change—technology. In the 1990s, the impact of technology on American corporations has been swift and undeniably evident. In contrast, the expected benefits from technology have followed with marked slowness. Businesses spent millions of dollars without seeing significant real return to their bottom lines.

As the turn of the century approaches, the need to make technology pay off will become more and more critical. In the next ten years, business managers will be faced with challenges to the very survival of their businesses. These challenges emerge from heightened competition, process change, and the speed of market dynamics. We stand, or slip, on the sand of a world in paradigm shift.

To meet these challenges, two approaches are needed: 1) using technology to enable the business, and 2) seeing technology as an investment strategy.

This book is a tool to help both the information systems manager (CIO) and the business manager (CEO) take on these challenges and do so as partners. We offer a new view of how each manager will impact the successful utilization of technology for business growth. Our theme, as we address the gut issues in technology management, is "Making It Simple."

This book can be viewed as follows:

- a road map to survival,
- a method for promoting a mind-set change, and
- a set of models for managing the process.

The information provided is a collection of the central concepts we've developed from our experience as two executives who survived many paradigm shifts. We are Ken Knight, educator, businessman, entrepreneur, and CEO survivor, and Bill Bysinger, technologist, pragmatist, entrepreneur, and CIO survivor.

Ken is the "big-picture" guy, a people person. Not thrilled to be in the company of computers, he is, nevertheless, appreciative of their value. Bill, on the other hand, is a computer expert with a vision for wider issues. He brings a wry smile and a teacher's heart to his life's work. Our collaboration has been dynamic. We're both excited to see how our experiences, from our separate perspectives, come together to give a full picture of the problem and its solutions. Together, we explain how the CEO's and the CIO's perspectives and skills can be blended for success.

We outline a process for communication, appreciation, and collaboration between these two necessary managers. This process enables the success of the organization by investing, deploying, integrating, and managing technology for business growth. Managers can take a first step toward working together in new ways by reading this book.

Designed as a reference piece, the book is useful as:

- a set of models that illustrate specific management methods;
- a handbook that shows how to meet business challenges by using technology as an enabler; and
- a collection of individual chapters that can be referred to during your continuing adventure managing the paradigm shift.

Both of us believe that this is a book like none before it. We get into the good, the bad, and the ugly. Most importantly, we show how a business executive and a technology executive can make a difference. This book provides insight into how you can leverage technology for return on investment. We've found the positive changes exciting and we want to pass the excitement on to you.

Our touchstone—the theme we'll return to—is the paradigm shift occurring in technology process. The theme has gone by the names "client/server," "information at your fingertips," "the virtual corporation," "reinventing the organization," or "reengineering the business." We believe that the most necessary shift is a "mind-set change in how to create success" through the collaboration of technology and business management practices.

However, in this time of rapid change in the late twentieth and early twenty-first century, one axiom remains true. As quoted from Barker in *The Paradigm Effect*, "When a paradigm shift happens, everything goes back to zero." In other words, the collective wisdom we've gained from our past experience is not valid as a guide to navigating the paradigm shift.

PROLOGUE

Surviving the Business Process Shift from the Business Manager's Viewpoint by Ken Knight

My experience with computers started in 1957 when I was an undergraduate at Yale University. I ventured down into the basement of the astronomy building to use the university's new IBM 650. I remember a room full of churning equipment that gave off a lot of heat. All this stuff was relegated to the basement.

Equipment considered unimportant then is now crucial to business survival. Over the year's, I have seen a reshaping of everything I was taught and had been teaching (in such schools as Stanford and the University of Texas at Austin). Almost all the "business facts" I taught as few as fifteen years ago are now irrelevant. Such momentous change is like the earth moving underfoot; it can cause great fear. When my world has been turned upside down, I wonder how I can land on my feet. I've experienced landing on my head—and it hurts.

The questions we ask in this changing technological environment include:

- How much should I really spend on computing?
- Who should manage the implementation of my technology?
- How do I make sure that my organization is using the most appropriate and latest technology?
- How can I determine if my technology expenditures provide a return to the business?
- How can I look to technology to develop a strategic advantage for my business?

I also remember how unforgiving that IBM 650 was. I entered my punched cards and set the digital switches to run my machine-language programs. I learned very quickly that computers were very good at following detailed instructions. This meant that if I made a program mistake, the computer would always make the same mistake every time the program ran. I also learned that, as a person who is enamored by the big picture, the rigorous detail of the computer was not for me.

As a result, I've looked to technologists to deal with all my computer issues as I developed my career as an educator, businessman, and entrepreneur. I reasoned that, after all, I'm a business manager—I hire technologists to do the computer stuff.

Today, I'm in a changed world. The computer is finding its way onto the desks of almost every employee in the organizations that I manage and advise. Even struggling charities are talking about networked systems, client/servers, and the Internet. Now that my world has changed, it's my turn to change.

I can no longer turn over my company's computing to a technologist and assume that she or he knows best. I need to learn to communicate clearly with those young computer whizzes to make sure that they fully understand my business processes.

As business managers, we have to manage the electronic wizardry with as much care as any other aspect of our business. Technology needs to be viewed as one more business process. Technology for technology's sake is nothing more than a very expensive toy—I've learned exactly how expensive on several occasions. My computer budget has become too big to ignore. I need to make sure that I am truly getting value from each dollar spent.

Several questions recur:

- How do I get my technologists to recognize that I want technology to enhance the productivity of my business?

- How do I get my technologist away from the technology long enough to understand my business problems?

- How do I deal with the fact that every month I hear of a new computer, new software, a new communications product, or a new service that renders obsolete what I purchased last month?

- How can I get all this technology (and the wizards that work with it) to stop creating unanticipated problems in my business?

Technological change is occurring at an ever-increasing rate. Computers, software, and communications technology can no longer be ignored, no matter how hard I try. These technologies are providing dramatic business advantages. They can increase productivity and create strategic product and service advantages. Surrounded by change and opportunity, we nervously try to steer clear of budget-busting nonsolutions.

More than anything, we need business solutions. We need technology that our employees can use as easily as they use their phones, cars, or televisions. We need to have proof that what is being developed will work when it's delivered. It must also be updated quickly and cheaply as business requirements change in our increasingly competitive markets. We are all experiencing the most radical reshaping of business processes, in America and worldwide. Technology is driving this revolution. We are participants in this change, and we need to make the technology work for us.

I'm a survivor of this technological onslaught. As I address the questions we've posed here, I hope to equip you with the information you need to be a survivor too.

As I have grown as a manager and educator, I have come around to the realization that my job is not to convey accurate factual knowledge. Managers in today's knowledge-based society cannot know everything necessary to make our organizations successful. Instead, my job is to help my people develop ways to think about and analyze the issues they face every day. Words like *mentor* or *coach* best describe what I strive to be.

I arrive at another important need: to trust my technologist. We must hire and work closely with people who are, at least in their field, far more knowledgeable than we are as managers. Dropping the notion that I must always be in control is not an easy prospect for me as a type-A manager. After all, isn't the manager supposed to tell his or her subordinates what to do and how to do it? (And isn't the teacher the ultimate purveyor of truth?) The manager's role has moved drastically away from this notion.

I have also discovered that truth is elusive. The generally accepted truths about managing information systems have shifted toward different principles that I don't completely comprehend. What works today will probably need to be changed tomorrow. Even more interesting, I've found that some of the old management skills and competencies that have been around for a very long time are becoming useful again.

I hope that my half of this book will communicate to you some of the insights gained from my experiences. After my share of challenges, I must admit that I've learned the most from my failures. As an educator, I want to help you to avoid my mistakes and learn more from your own failures. Don't worry—if you haven't made mistakes already, you will; you'll make plenty of them.

Using these fancy information and knowledge systems is exciting. It's a lucky thing that you don't need to know everything to succeed with them.

PROLOGUE

Surviving the Business Process Shift from the Information System Manager's Viewpoint
by Bill Bysinger

I have been in the information systems business since card decks were the norm. I have used **COBOL**, **FORTRAN**, **PL/1**, and **Basic**. I know how to spell **ALGOL**, Snobal, Ada, and Pascal. The current reality for those of us in positions as CIOs, MIS directors, or managers of information systems is that such knowledge doesn't count for much in our work.

What counts in information systems (IS) management today is not what we know about technology or that we were good programmers; what counts is: Can we sell our ideas to business management? Can we justify the money we need to be effective in the delivery of technology and information to the corporation?

Instead of how to program, the new how-tos in our jobs are:

- How do I get the budget I need without getting beat up?
- How do I transform my MIS organization from a cost generator into a revenue contributor?
- How do I convince the business managers in my company that I'm there to help them be more productive?
- How do I wade through the confusion of technology that presents itself to me every day?
- How can I make sense out of all this and be successful in the profession we call information systems? More specifically, how can I be successful in the volatile position of directing the use of information technology in my company?

We're part of the fastest-growing industry in the world. Our profession has a higher turnover rate than air-traffic controllers. We're striving to survive in a job that has one of the highest mortality rates of any management position in the late 1980s. And this rate has risen even higher in the 1990s.

At the same time, we're coping with the blurring pace of technology and the dynamics of information delivery, plus defending our budgets and, if that isn't enough, trying to prove to the company that we can contribute. We're questioned constantly about our organization's abilities to deliver. Meanwhile, one of our primary jobs is to make the MIS organization invisible.

This book should help you not only to survive but to have fun in the process. I have come to believe that my job is more educator than technologist. I need to interpret the use of information systems for business advantage rather than to define the systems. The education process happens at all levels. These chapters will draw a road map for educating your company so they can start to recognize the value you and your organization offer. Through this education, you'll succeed, your company will prosper, and your staff will be charged up and challenged to continue contributing to the growth of your company.

CHAPTER 1

A Different Agenda: What Does the Business Manager Need to Know? by Ken Knight

"As a Systems person, I continue to struggle with business people who expect my people to understand their business. We barely have enough time to deal with the day to day, much less get educated on the business."

"I wish the managers and executives in this company would take ownership for some of the systems we develop and acquire for them. They only want us to build it faster, make it better, and we'll call you when we have problems."

"I need the formula for how I can get the business involved with technology and have them begin to understand that I want to help them, not just react to problems."

All Information Systems Managers want to be more relevant to the business. They struggle to know what it will take to have the business understand that they can provide value. The journey through this book will help make that unknown become more known between both business and MIS management.

In the first chapter of the book Ken deals with five major issues that are critical to successfully implement and use technology in business. These are:

1. *Business responsibility to technology based decision*
2. *Business knowledge of those implementing technology in the business*
3. *Successful communication between the business and systems people*
4. *Ownership of the technology process that is applied to the business*
5. *Customers both internal and external and how their needs can be met through systems and technologies applied to the business*

The lessons learned by Ken are very appropriate to addressing each of these issues.

Bill Bysinger

In discussions with friends in management, I hear the repeated question, "Am I ever going to be able to manage my information and communications technology?" We read business magazines full of articles about how the burgeoning information highway will change the way we do business. This glorious electronic world sounds great. But every time I try a new technology, my business falls into a crisis that gobbles up lots of time and money.

A colleague of mine who is a senior executive of a large public company complained "Ken, I'm at my wits' end. I've been trying to get my MIS staff to complete implementation of our new, integrated, customer-order-processing system for my mail-order catalog business. But MIS is killing us! They just don't get it! We've been working on this for over three years now, and all that seems to happen is that costs grow exponentially and the completion date gets put off for another four to six months." I joked, "Sounds like the Denver Airport's state-of-the-art automated baggage system. After so many delays, it seems like it will never work!"

That same senior executive also told me that his mind goes blank when computers and MIS are mentioned. He informed me that he leaves all the computer and technology matters to his chief information officer (CIO).

At the other extreme is my twenty-one-year-old daughter. Jennifer grabs up new programs like Autocad and Quick Books and attacks them as if they were new computer games. Her willingness to plunge into any project, added to her can-do attitude, helps her master any PC-based software application in short order. Many of our kids see the computer as an extension of themselves. For Jennifer, moving through the help screens is just another fun challenge.

COMPUTERS BECOME CRITICAL TO OUR BUSINESSES

Computers are technological devices. As they become increasingly central to, and critical in, the operation of our organization, we become subject to interruption as a result of technical problems. If we depend more and more on the information highway, we will subject ourselves to potential disruption.

For example, I spent a Monday evening in the airport in Ontario, California, near our home. My wife, Ann, and

I were seeing Jennifer off to Seattle. We had arrived one hour early because freeway traffic had been a lot lighter than usual for southern California.

I stopped by the Southwest Airlines ticket counter to purchase a ticket for a future trip. The agent, Sally, confirmed my reservation and entered the command to print the ticket. Nothing happened. "The computers are down," Sally told us. "We can't write tickets by hand. It will only take a minute to print your ticket after the computers come up. Would you like to wait here?" We spent the next twenty minutes chatting pleasantly.

The wait was not so pleasant for the ever-lengthening line of anxious customers trying to catch their flights. The manager on duty called Southwest management in California and then their operations center in Texas. No one seemed to know if the problem was a computer problem or a communications problem or if it was local or at the corporate computer headquarters. The growing line of customers just wanted to know if they were going to get their tickets or miss their flights.

After seeing Jennifer off, Ann and I returned thirty minutes later to a line of over a hundred worried people. No one had been serviced. I checked at Sally's counter, where my record was still on the screen, and asked if Southwest could mail me the ticket. The answer was no because I was using a coupon. Five minutes later, Sally's supervisor said, "Yeah, it's active." One minute later, my ticket was printed and in my hand.

These problems need to be anticipated and planned for. We will not have a zero-defect information system, certainly not in the next few years. In addition, our systems will not be secure. Hackers and technology spies will develop ways to access our critical information and inject new viruses.

The pressing question in the mind of the computer skeptic or computer illiterate is: Can I ever manage my computer and communications technology?

MIS SHOULD STAND FOR "MAKE IT SIMPLE"

Bill and I summarize the approach that works consistently for us as: MIS needs to stand for "Make it simple!" We are convinced that, with an effective approach, you can. That's easy to say. You'll see how easy it is to do as we explain our simple methodology in these chapters.

Reviewing my career, I now realize that, although I loved computers, I left the development and implementation of their applications to my computer experts. I thought, after all that I was the general manager and that the technologist knew best about technology. *Wrong*!

THE MANAGER OWNS THE BUSINESS PROCESS

Our model starts off with a simple assumption: The business manager is the owner of the business process. It is his responsibility to see that every aspect of the business operates successfully.

My computer people see the business manager as their customer. He takes the customer role for two reasons. First, like most customers, he has the money. Second, he knows what the problem is that he wants solved by his computer and communications technology.

The people who work for him are the front-line workers. These employees are the ones who fully understand the intricacies of the company's business process. The front-line workers will have to make the computerized information systems generate revenues, produce products and services, deliver them to customers, and provide customers with necessary follow-up and service. These front-line employees and the other managers in the organization define what needs to be facilitated by the firm's investment in technology.

This sounds like a simple concept, and it is. But I didn't recognize it when I started out in the early 1970s as one of the founders of a venture called Lex Systems. My programming staff led me to believe that programming was their domain; I, as president, should leave them alone. So I did. What a mistake! Away they rushed to their own little corner to generate what they thought we needed.

They did produce a great piece of technical art. The key programmer used every COBOL trick he had ever learned to make an elegant, fast program. He went on to write new codes, leaving it to others to test the programs.

Then the customers requested changes to his program, which slowed my expert programmer down a great deal. His approach had been to get excited about programming and launch into it with only a cursory knowledge of what the customer really needed. He had constructed what he thought they needed. He didn't understand the business problems and process in adequate depth. He didn't take the time to involve any of his customers in defining the information system.

At that point, I made the decision to step in and make some changes. I had hoped that the requested changes could be implemented with ease, but I was wrong. Because my expert programmer had constructed such an elegant program, the other programmers didn't understand the program or its documentation. Every change was extremely difficult and costly.

The good news is that I finally got the program to do what the business process owners wanted. But I had learned a lesson the hard way: Always involve the owners of the business process in all steps of the creation and implementation of a computerized information system, from the development of the problem statement to program testing.

THE MANAGER CONTROLS TECHNOLOGY

It is important the manager takes responsibility for technology and its uses in the organization. For most companies today, computers represent a major investment. The organization's investment in computers is as critical as the time and money put into other diverse areas, such as sales campaigns, new manufacturing facilities, acquisition of capital, product development, or employee training and development.

The problem that I encountered was that it was so easy to turn over the development of my technology systems to my computer specialist and go on to other aspects of the business that I enjoyed more and understood better. This approach didn't work back in the 1970s and it works even less today as automated information systems become mission-critical aspects of every organization.

What do I mean by "mission-critical?" Simply this: If a mission-critical information system doesn't work, my organization is unable to deliver a product or service that the customer expects at an acceptable quality and cost. To put it more bluntly, if the information system doesn't perform, the organization will cease to exist.

THE BUSINESS MANAGER IS THE CUSTOMER

The business manager now has no choice but to get involved in all aspects of the creation and implementation of the organization's computerized systems. If he can't or won't, he shouldn't be the business process owner—he should resign as the president or chief executive officer. I underline here that I am not saying that the business manager should do the systems analysis or programming; he should just understand what is being developed and why. Also, I am not saying that he should understand as much about the technology as those who work for him do.

Here we have two essential points to remember. First, the business manager controls the money. Second, the business manager must not assume that the technologist knows the answer. The people closest to the action have the best understanding of the problem or function in the business process that the technology will address. The owners of the business process are the customers. The computer technologist is the supplier. The technologist must first listen to the business manager. Then the business manager must work with the information systems people from the creation to the deployment of the technology. The technology is there only to enhance jobs and business process.

We just took the first step in understanding how MIS can mean "Make it simple."

THE INFORMATION HIGHWAY RUNS THROUGH EACH ORGANIZATION

Business stands at the brink of meaningful exploitation of computing and communications. Our technical capability to create cost and productivity improvements will grow more in the next ten years than it has in the past forty years, since computers appeared on the scene. Managers need to get on board. It is going to be an exciting ride as we see all aspects of our business processes facilitated by computers and communications. We need to address this evolving enhancement of our organizations with as much effort, enthusiasm, and rigor as we apply to other changes and investments.

The information highway is being built as you read these words. Construction crews are inside our organizations. The highway can connect our organizations to the rest of the world, making our organizations far more productive, profitable, and valuable. This same information highway could also represent a rapid route to oblivion.

Now let's look at some of the dramatic changes that are possible even today.

MANAGING IN THE TWENTY-FIRST CENTURY: WHAT A MANAGER NEEDS TO REMEMBER ABOUT TECHNOLOGY

1. The emerging *information highway* will change the way every organization operates.

2. Computers are *critical* to every business.

3. Information systems are not to be left to the "techies."

4. MIS should stand for both "Make it simple" and management information systems.

5. Get started in your information systems evolution (revolution) by remembering that you (the manager) own the business process.

6. The manager must control how technology is utilized.

7. The business manager is the information technologist's customer and needs to act like a customer.

CHAPTER 2

A Different Agenda: Discovering Customers
by Bill Bysinger

"I will show you what it does and how it works when I finish the programming. Just leave me alone so that I can finish."

"We have shut down your server for two days to install faster hardware."

"I know I said the WWW site would be up by the 15th, but I am trying to get the colors, pictures and sound track just right. This requires a lot of fine tuning. It is not my problem that you published the web site address in our new ads."

"You did what????!!!"

When it comes to the business processes, many technologists haven't got a clue. They view the world from the technology vantage and have no understanding what is really needed or what the consequences of their actions are.

Part of this is my problem. Often I am not willing to spend the time to take charge and make sure that the technologist understands the problem and how it needs to be solved.

> *In this chapter, Bill addresses a major concern of mine. I'm the technologist's customer,(and request that I be treated as such). Bill builds on my statement in Chapter 1 that managers cannot relinquish control of an organization's use of computers, communication and information systems technology. Bill discusses why both the technologist and the business manager must work closely together. He describes the business manager in that working relationship as the technologist's customer, while the business manager controls the money.*
>
> *Ken Knight*

We're at the beginning of our journey toward *making it simple*. We're navigating the area where business and technology intersect. Our periscope is pointed at one key target: the recipients of our product—our customers.

Customers are those internal folks who need IS tools and the information generated by our systems. (External customers are remote from IS, unless you are supplying a product to them directly.)

When I was a young MBA student, I believed that my goal was "to understand the mission-critical success factors of the organization." In the real world of users, I found that this goal was too lofty. I first needed to identify my audience. Next, I needed to find out what they did. Then I could determine what they needed from me to be more productive.

Too many of the systems I have delivered over the years had no real customer (sponsor) who cared. Or, by the time the system was delivered, the customers had changed because the business had drifted into some other area not yet defined.

TALK TO THE MANAGERS

A few years ago, I took a position as the director of information systems for a fast-growing high-tech company. For the first ninety days in my position, I wandered around the company trying to talk to anyone who had responsibility for anyone other than themselves.

Interesting things began to happen. Most of the people I spent time with were not in information systems. I'm sure my staff thought I was a little goofy. But I learned a lot about how IS was perceived, and especially how the businesspeople believed IS was contributing.

Several of them asked me, "Why meet with *me*? I get nothing of value from the mainframe," or, "Are you just trying to waste my time?"

My response was, "I'm here to see if you are frustrated because you don't have the tools or information to do your job. If so, what tools and information do you need?" I was trying to determine where the pressure points were in the business.

From my wanderings, I gained a better understanding of what technology isn't doing and what it should do. I also formed perceptions of what kinds of information were needed but were unavailable.

I'm proud that not once did I utter the words from my 1970s MBA training: "mission-critical success factors." People normally do not know how to respond to, and may even be offended, by this phrase. Instead, I tried what-if scenarios. For example: "What if I could get you that data, merge it with the most recent related data, and generate this type of report or mail message?" A concrete illustration, like a picture, is worth a thousand words.

FIND YOUR CUSTOMERS

In the early 1980s, I was a vice president of information systems for a services company. In this position, I had some moderate success with the delivery of business systems based on a new technology called DEC VAX. As a result of my success, DEC (Digital Equipment Corporation) asked me to join them to help their salespeople sell to technology executives like me. They wanted me to talk to, and work with, their salespeople to help them understand the business of large-scale commercial computing and how to market products successfully in business settings. Since I had never sold anything, and I needed first to understand the sales process. I made an unusual request—that I go to sales school and become a salesperson for a year. Sometimes the best thing you can do to help solve someone's problems is to walk in that person's shoes.

I learned a lot that year. One of the most important lessons was how to find customers. That's right—an information systems manager finds customers.

Information systems is typically weak on finding the right customers. The right customers are the ones who make us successful in the business. For too long we have measured our success by past formulas. Business success is better judged by our ability to respond more quickly to future opportunities. Most information systems organizations concentrate on projects that have no real business value.

My target has always been the customer who is bleeding the most. I determine who needs a solution either to win new business or to increase the ability to respond to business change.

KNOW YOUR CUSTOMERS

I believe my success depends greatly on understanding my customer. Without good customers, I will not survive. Even if I do survive, I'll be ineffective for the company. So, following a new agenda in IS begins with identifying the customer because 1) *the customer has the money*, and 2) *the customer needs us*.

Think about how you identify customers. Who are the customers in your business? Which factors influence how you help them? Here's a quick sketch:

- Senior business managers control the money.
- Business unit managers have the problems.
- Supervisors need the tools.

- Front-line users understand the process.

Each of these customers is important. You need to play different roles with each. The whole process is a "sale," which begins the minute you uncover an opportunity for IS to make a difference. Information systems must make a difference to the customer, not just automate an activity. In sales training, this is called pioneering for prospects.

From my time in sales, I learned that good salespeople are great systems analysts. I would love to send all my IS people to sales training. There is no better way to gain an understanding of the real need (requirements) of the customer (user).

Let's go back to my stroll through my high-technology company as director of information systems. My wanderings made me aware of many things. I discovered customers and their needs. But I also found that customers' perceptions of IS and technology were important for me to see and hear.

It's always a challenge being the IS guy in a technology company. Everyone in the company believes she or he knows more than you about technology and IS. You learn to be humble.

LISTEN TO YOUR CUSTOMERS

Mindful of the need for humility, I did a great deal of listening. I found that the greater my understanding of my customers, the more relevant my efforts were to the company. I understood my customers better by putting myself in their place. I asked myself: What do I appreciate in a salesperson? I like a knowledgeable salesperson who listens to me and tries to understand and provide useful suggestions for my needs.

As an MIS person, you'll find that the key to understanding your customer is in asking the right questions. Consider how often we ask the wrong questions. Or we wait for someone to bring an issue to us, and then we determine if it is important enough for us to work on it.

I believe that the mission of the CIO and IS managers is to find the right customers. I also think that we benefit from being humble in the process. This approach may seem radical to you but, as you read this book, you will continue to observe my unconventional approach to technology management as a CIO.

INTERVIEW YOUR CUSTOMERS

Here's a quick test to check your current approach. Which questions do you ask your customers?

- "Can you show me your business plan?" *Wrong*. They usually don't have one. Even if they do, they'd rather not expose it to you.
- "How do you measure organizational success?" *Correct*. Actionable.
- "What are your key objectives for the next year?" *Wrong*. They probably don't have any.

- "What are your measures for a good performance review?" *Correct.* Discrete, measurable.
- "What are your strategic initiatives?" *Wrong.* Too big.
- "How will you attain your bonus?" *Correct.* Close to the heart.

CREATE MANAGEMENT AND IS BONDING

Armed with the answers to these questions, I would be able to target the issues that IS should assist in addressing.

Since this must be a reciprocal relationship, my customers should also have some commitment to me. In a later chapter, we'll see an example of this reciprocity in a situation that catapulted my IS organization into the funding of global client/server delivery in 1989.

In that year, I found a customer organization that needed help in the order-processing department. Their computer users found themselves unable to deliver on their mission, which was to process a certain amount of orders per day. I began my diagnosis by sitting down to process an order. With the existing systems, the process was so convoluted that it was almost impossible to process orders efficiently. The system was four years old, a classic example of a system that had not changed with the business.

In a high-technology company, unless the product leaves the dock, its revenue is not realized, no matter how much product is sold. Since we were a publicly held company, order-processing problems had a major impact on stock value and earnings per share.

To help unclog this bottleneck, the department manager and I went to the vice president of the division responsible for processing orders. This VP's bonus, credibility, and organizational effectiveness, not to mention the company's quarterly earnings results, were riding on our ability to solve this problem.

The three of us took a new approach. The vice president, the department manager, and I entered into a cooperative project in which each of us held significant risk and responsibility. Our project later became the model for IS-and-customer-shared-risk projects in the company.

Our need was to make the problem of order processing go away by increasing our ability to process orders. We wanted to achieve these results in less than five months.

The customer was viewed as follows:

- The vice president: the project sponsor; also the one with the money

- The department manager: the process-change manager, who also commits resources

- The supervisors: the keepers of the process; those who believe most in the need for change

- The front-line users: those who lived the process and wanted change most

Information systems was the supplier. Our responsibilities were as follows:

- As corporate IS director, I became the project manager
- IS provided development resources
- We borrowed some user-interface development resources from the end-user department
- IS provided the development tools

The project model looked like this:

- We planned to complete it in ninety days
- The project would introduce new technology into our company (a new user interface and mainframe connection)
- The VP would provide the money to underwrite the project
- The VP and IS director would collaborate on a return-on-investment (ROI) model that would yield at least a threefold increase in order processing, achieved in less than twelve months

Here are the results:

- We completed the project in eighty-nine days
- We implemented new software technology on desktops
- We integrated mainframe technology with front-end user-interface transactions
- A new development model was used for all systems
- We achieved a fivefold ROI in six months

This list doesn't mention the best results from this project. The division vice president became a marketing spokesman for IS. Our company turned to this project as a model of building success with IS. We see from this example how we need to view customer relationships.

Customers are the people with the money and the need. The lifeblood of IS is picking customers and making them successful. If this is done right, IS never has to worry about funding or about relevance to the business. If IS can't strive for the customer's success, then IS shouldn't be funded. In addition, IS and the customer will continue struggling to succeed.

The chapters that follow will provide more in-depth insight into how this process can be made successful without your customers creating havoc or acquiring excessive expectations of IS.

CHECKLIST FOR PIONEERING FOR CUSTOMERS

FACTS:

- MIS has no money
- MIS uses other people's money
- MIS must have customers
- Customers expect value for money invested

How to Identify a Valued Customer

1. Know who potential customers are:
   - Senior business managers control money
   - Business unit managers have the business problems
   - Supervisors need the tools
   - Front-line users understand the process
2. Listen to the each level of customer for cues.
3. Ask open-ended questions:
   - How do you measure organizational success?
   - What are your measures for good performance?
   - How will you attain your periodic (annual, quarterly) bonus?
   - What data is critical to your process?
   - Who generates that data?
4. Understand clearly the output of the sponsor organization's business (for example: orders, information, products, inventory).
5. Identify a real problem or process improvement that can do one of the following for the organization:
   - Create better profit margins (process improvement)
   - Generate more revenue for the business (higher productivity)

- Create an opportunity to enter a new business (new process, product, or service)
6. Define a project that addresses the business issues and can be completed in six to nine months through the use of technology and systems
7. Make sure you have a high-level sponsor who has the money.
8. Make sure the sponsor has resources to commit to work the project.
9. Determine a cost of the product (the project you deliver).
10. Negotiate a return with the sponsor to justify the dollars invested (should be a ratio of at least 2:1 or 3:1, payable in twelve to eighteen months after the project is completed and in production).

CHAPTER 3

Folklore and Fairy Tale: The Advantage from Technology

by Ken Knight

"I am really tired of having my MIS team be the only ones really committed to the success of these projects. It always seems like everything else is more important than the projects we have been asked to do for the company."

"I wish the user departments would commit the resources necessary to make this systems project a success. How can I get them involved, what do we need to do to build the right team?"

"We need project teams but the users appear to have different agendas than MIS."

On too many systems and technology projects, MIS feels like they are alone to fail; they feel the business is off doing other more important things, even though the projects that MIS is usually involved with directly impacts the efficiency and performance of the business operation.

In this chapter Ken address the importance of business process and teamwork. It is about keeping your eye on the ball and making sure that all who are impacted by the change are considered. It is also about the importance of making sure that everyone is pulling in the right direction.

Bill Bysinger

Now that we've better identified IS customers, I see that, as a customer of IS, I need to look at my expectations. During much of my experience managing and educating about management, I've assumed that technology could solve all my problems. I've also assumed that employees create all the problems I encounter.

Having used computer systems extensively over the past twenty-five years, I fully recognize that the organizations I've been involved with couldn't function today without modern computers and communications technology. The thought of writing this manuscript without the flexibility of my PC horrifies me. My PC makes it easy to correct my not-so-occasional random strokes. Also, my spelling, like my distant cousin Dan Quayle's, leaves a lot to be desired. My administrative assistant is right—"A spell check is a necessity."

Development of personal computers has enhanced the abilities of the individual worker enormously. I take advantage by familiarizing myself with a dozen programs I use every week. Also, I don't hesitate to learn the new versions as soon as they're released. Unfortunately, I can't say the same about the corporate-wide automated systems in my organizations. The split between PCs and mainframes has been evident.

THE INDIVIDUAL USER SEES HIS WORLD AS ORDERED

As an individual user, I both create and clean up my own mess. I store some information on my PC, but I keep some of the process that I am trying to accomplish in my head. Because I'm the only user of the information on my PC and in my head, it's all instantly available to me. I'm in control, so I decide how much I need to document. I name a file whatever I want to because I am the only one who will retrieve it. I can be as sloppy as I can stand.

This important attribute of the PC has contributed to its high impact on business today. The isolated user can customize his or her use to suit his or her thought patterns without coordinating with anyone else's preferences. As such, the PC in the individual user mode has become an enormous enhancer of productivity.

Individual users enjoy being in control of their own space. I like to move any files I need onto my own PC, where I can manipulate them as I see fit. Life just seems more comfortable when I'm in control. I know where everything is. I know were I left off when I shut the PC down yesterday afternoon. My world is in order, that is, it's in *my* order.

Today, organizations are moving quickly from central computing to distributed PCs, putting the individual user in control. This migration is widely celebrated because it moves data and information resources to each individual PC user. Our lives as users become easier, in principle, because we are now in control. We've eliminated our dependence on others. My independence is a plus as long as my work doesn't become a critical input for one of my colleagues.

OTHERS SEE MY PC WORLD AS CHAOTIC

If a colleague needs one of my files—a spreadsheet, for example—our worlds become a lot more complicated. My colleague must first figure out how to access my data. Then she or he has to figure out what I've given her/him, for example, what my abbreviations stand for.

My coworker, who is now dependent on understanding my thought and work processes, has a daunting task because I've been working in my own idiosyncratic fashion. I haven't provided documentation explaining my processes. To a colleague, my order may look like chaos.

I encountered a similar level of confusion working with a small company. I tried to understand the information in a computerized accounting system without benefit of the knowledge of the clerk who set up the system. The originator had done nothing wrong. No one tried to generate confusion. But it is just the tendency of individual PC users to merge their idiosyncratic thought patterns with the work they originate.

The PC is like a double-edged sword. It gives us technology that allows us to perform according to our own processes. But it makes organizational life more difficult as we need each other's information to accomplish our jobs.

The current shift away from the enterprise mainframe indicates, among other things, dissatisfaction with a rigid structure controlled by a centralized management information systems/computer information systems staff. At the same time, in the shift toward PC-based systems, business users generally acknowledged the need to integrate these individual systems into a distributed system with shared data and processes.

COMPUTERIZED INFORMATION SYSTEMS CAN CREATE A STRATEGIC BUSINESS ADVANTAGE

Choosing the right system is even more important in light of its strategic value to the company. The computer can be a source of strategic advantage to the organization. Let's look at some specific examples of strategic advantage.

Federal Express uses its computerized information system to generate a strategic advantage. Ten years ago, when visiting the Reno, Nevada area, I was expecting a critical package. Early in the evening, I found out that there was no delivery until five p.m. The package was addressed to Incline Village, Nevada.

I called Federal Express to say that I needed earlier delivery. Was it possible? Their answer was, "No problem!" They could tell me that the package was now on a plane en route to Memphis. They could pull it and have it available for me to pick up at eight a.m. at the Federal Express terminal at the Reno Airport. Not quite believing all this, I showed up at the Federal Express Reno terminal and asked for my package. To my astonishment, it was handed to me immediately.

How did FedEx do that? Since the company was established, Federal Express has used an advanced computer and communications system to create a clear strategic advantage over their competition. With hand-held scanners, FedEx is able to track each package every time it is handled. Knowing where a package is at any point in time allows FedEx to provide a valuable customer service. After this experience, I became a loyal Federal Express customer.

WalMart also uses information technology to create a competitive advantage. Via a combination of computers and communications technology, WalMart interacts directly with its suppliers to coordinate inventory control. Each purchase from suppliers is transacted electronically. Any vendor wanting to do business with WalMart must agree to WalMart's electronic interface.

L.L. Bean surprised me last year. I called to place an order from its catalog. Before I said anything, the representative started the conversation with, "May we help you, Mr. Knight?" and went on to ask, "Were you satisfied with the shirt you purchased recently?" After I placed my new order, the representative asked if I wanted it delivered to my home address, which he had in front of him. Also, did I wish to use my MasterCard and second-day, air-express shipment again?

L.L. Bean and other mail-order companies store key customer information on their computer systems. How did this conversation make me feel as a customer? After I hung up, I felt that L.L. Bean was interested enough in me to develop the ability to speed up my order. My conclusion: L.L. Bean appreciates its customers.

The uses of computer technology by Federal Express, WalMart, and L.L. Bean that benefit me as a customer are evidence of underlying successful business processes. In each case, the companies understood their business processes and how to improve them. Then they applied technology in a way that enhanced their business processes. Because their improvements benefit me as a customer, I'm impressed that they're interested in me. Their customer awareness makes their product or service more valuable to me. Because of the added value I receive, I would even be willing to pay more.

SERVICE, NOT TECHNOLOGY, CREATES VALUE

Here is an important distinction, the technology itself creates no value to the customer. Only if the technology improves the product or service to the customer does he or she sense an improvement, which indicates that the technology has improved the business process. Therefore, as the business manager, I must start my analysis of how technology can enable my business by looking at my business process.

Too often, the order of events is the other way around. For instance, my technologist gets all excited about certain technological advances and wants to rush them into my organization. All too often, the excitement is contagious. I approve the new systems, and as a result, I pay dearly both in time and money.

For instance, in the late 1970s and early 1980s, I was working with my brother-in-law, who was president of a small, family-owned wood products business in a town called Joseph, Oregon. Somehow, a technologist got him excited about the things a computer could do for his company. He told us that a computer was the obvious tool of choice. It could do wonders for the productivity of our staff architect, who designed homes, supplied finished drawings, estimated prices and costs, and performed some accounting functions. As chairman of the board, I agreed with my brother-in-law that we would purchase a fancy minicomputer.

Joseph, Oregon has many fine qualities. The town is located in beautiful, mountainous Wallowa County, with forest products and recreation as its major industries. Unfortunately, support for minicomputers is scarce in Joseph. Local technologists played with the computer for a few years. Our investment generated little more than grief for our company, and we spent a lot of money.

In retrospect, we saw clearly that we had not addressed how the proposed computing technology would support a critical business process. Instead, we fixated on the glory of the computer. After all, we thought, successful companies had computers, didn't they? Our assumption that a computer would show the world that we were successful turned out to be an expensive mistake.

When I talk to managers, I find that many of them purchase technology because they feel it's the "in" thing to do. I hear, "Computers solve all management problems, don't they?" I answer with an emphatic "No!" We need to look at the business process first. Then we use technology if, and only if, it enhances the business process.

CAN TECHNOLOGY CREATE VALUE FOR YOUR ORGANIZATION?

How do technology and information systems fit into an organization? Sounds like a simple question, yet I find few organizations that state clearly, and understand the mission and objectives of the information systems group. The heart of these missions and objectives is on the support IS provides the business process. How does it make the organization more effective and efficient? The information technology teams should be creating and implementing technology that increases the revenues or profitability of the firm or that generates new business, products, or services for the firm.

I received a phone call last year from the owner of a small (twenty-five-person) metal shop in Seattle. There are a lot of these shops in the metropolitan area because of the proximity of large customers like Boeing and Paccar (manufacturer of Kenworth trucks). The management team comprised of the owner and his wife, wanted to see if a group of Seattle Pacific University students could work with their firm to install a network that would connect the company's PCs and allow the organization to connect electronically with customers.

When I visited the firm, I brought along an undergraduate student who was familiar with networks. Three things became clear. First, the owner-manager had not conceived exactly how the proposed network would fit into and improve his business operations. In fact, he really didn't know much about computers, although he had three 1992 IBM class 286s in the firm. He had been talked into acquiring the computer network by a computer consultant he had hired. Second, he had no real business process needs at this time for the shared-file or customer-communications requirements he was looking for. Third, he had no understanding of the original cost or the network maintenance that would be required to establish the computer network he desired.

SEATTLE TWENTY-FIVE-PERSON METAL FABRICATOR

"PCs Don't Really Cost Much, Do They?"

The owner-manager thought that the local area network could be setup with his existing equipment, the purchase of two more PCs, and a few hundred dollars of new software. His view was that moving from manual paper to electronic order entry, manufacturing, inventory, and billing systems and then integrating those into his computerized accounting system would cost less than $5,000. He also thought that using this system would require no training and that, once the system was purchased, it would have no continuing costs.

My student and I estimated that the cost to establish a local area network to tie all the firm's computers together and develop "new" applications to have the network track the work as it progresses through the shop would be as follows:

Process analysis to specify the applications	$30,000
Computer upgrades and new equipment	$15,000
PC and network software	$12,500
Installation	$10,000
Employee training/coaching on the system's operations	$20,000
	$87,500
Annual systems maintenance and upgrades	$20,000

This story had a happy ending. When we spelled out the full cost of establishing the proposed network and the ongoing maintenance that would be required, the husband-and-wife team decided to pass on the network. Before they make another technological move, they'll devote themselves to understanding their business process and how it must change to meet the changing needs of their customers. Then a plan will be created that includes the timing of a future computer network that focuses on enhancing the firm's customer service.

IT CREATED VALUE FOR SMALL ORGANIZATIONS

Technology is creating a strategic advantage and becoming widely accepted in surprising places. Most of the businessmen I talk with believe that information systems only make a difference in large corporations. From my wanderings around the world, I find that nothing could be farther from the truth. In fact, the explosion of information technologies is having its biggest impact on small organizations and individuals.

Third World Missionaries Find IS Creating Value

In the winter of 1995, I was present at a conference of missionary organizations and missionaries. These organizations and individuals worked primarily in Third World countries. To my surprise, they all arrived equipped with laptop computers. These missionaries were sophisticated users of e-mail, faxes, and all sorts of electronic communication.

These missionary organizations were spread throughout the world, operating as virtual organizations! When I looked into it further, I saw why these organizations and individuals were such advocates of portable PCs and electronic communication: The technology really improved their business processes. Information technology made a very tangible improvement in how they accomplished their work, their success rate, and their ability to evaluate their progress. Working in the developing world, they were removed from face-to-face contacts with the rest of their organization. Mail and telephone communications were difficult and subject to government security interception. But computer electronic communications were one-third to one-tenth the cost of telephone communications in the Third World, and e-mail messages can be encrypted to ensure their privacy.

Sophisticated computer communications created a clear strategic advantage for these missionary organizations and their missionaries. These organizations are low-budget. These people aren't technologists; they are men and women out in the field trying to make a difference among the poorest people in the world.

Missionaries have bought into the use of sophisticated computers and digital communication. They are on the cutting edge in their use of the information highway. Computers and the electronic organization really make a difference in their lives. They aren't reluctant to use technology because it is to their strategic advantage.

The Virtual Organization Created with Information Technology

I observed another small organization that uses information systems to their strategic advantage—the Toles Company. George Toles runs a successful advertising agency. He works out of his house with help from his wife. The Toles company has clients both big and small. They stay with him—testimony to his success. The Toles Company is a virtual organization. It makes no difference where any of the employees, suppliers, or customers work. They are connected electronically and work without a "fixed site-specific office." The Toles Company has gotten on board the information highway, which creates great value for George and those individuals and organizations he works with.

George used to have a much larger organization in a downtown office. He gave up that traditional office for a virtual organization connected electronically to other electronically sophisticated professionals. Together, they provide the same services as other large advertising agencies but without the usual large overhead. George works with graphic designers, artists, writers, media buyers, video directors, cameramen, musicians, production crews, and so forth, all electronically. He keeps in constant communication with his customers and production team through desk-based and portable PCs. He has a virtual organization connected via digital computer communication.

He loves it. He told me that his life is much more productive and enjoyable with the advent of computer-to-computer, e-mail, voice mail, and fax communication. His information system technology provides the key to his whole operation and represents his strategic advantage over his larger competitors.

I wouldn't expect a people person like George to love technology. He doesn't, but he loves what the technology allows him to accomplish. He uses technology to enhance his business process. The technology increases his revenues and profits and provides business services he couldn't otherwise perform.

Another Example of the Evolving Information Technology: The Web Revolution

Whereas the Internet has been around for almost three decades, the development of Mosaic and other Internet browsers, has opened up the electronic highway to millions of us. There has never been a technology that has experienced growth as explosive as that of the Internet and its World Wide Web. This is a technology that allows computers of all types to talk with one another.

Although this technology is still in its infancy, we already know that it will dramatically change how all businesses operate. This information highway is not a fairy tale. We've already read and heard the stories of the start-up firm in Washington State that sold $2 million in stock over the Internet. Or the heartwarming story of an East Coast doctor who was unable to find a suitable bone marrow donor through conventional medical channels but did so within one week after setting up his WWW site to find that rare bone marrow match.

As a manager, I must be enamored of the World Wide Web (WWW). Every knowledgeable manager I meet believes it will almost immediately change how his or her organization functions. These managers are planning, developing, or implementing new internal communications networks, called "intranets," in their organizations. Intranets are internal networks that compare to the popular Internet. With intranets, firms no longer need to print internal telephone directories, employee manuals, training manuals, personnel policies, price and inventory lists, and much of the other existing internal organizational documents. They will make them available to those who have access to that information on all their local personal computers through the firm's intranet. The information will be the latest. I cannot say how many times I have struggled to find a telephone number, only to discover that I was using a telephone directory that was several years old or that the entries in a current directory were already out-of-date. Intranet directories can be updated at any time.

Most of us will agree that the rate of technological change is accelerating. The cry that I continually hear from my manager friends is, "Help! "How do I deal with this change? Where can I start?"

THE PROCESS IS THE PROBLEM

Information systems that were developed years ago are almost always based on old business processes. Although the business has changed over the years, when a new information system involving newer technology is implemented, changes in the business process that have occurred over the years are usually not reexamined. The resulting information systems are called *legacy systems*.

Legacy systems were developed years ago. They match the business process needs of yesterday. They were written in old computer languages and may run on obsolete computers. Programs for legacy systems were written and modified with little documentation by staff who left the company long ago. Keeping such systems running costs a great deal in dollars and labor.

I often encounter legacy systems as I help companies in my roles as consultant and business school dean. Without exception, every major corporation I have visited has legacy systems and, for many, these systems represent the majority of their information systems. (I will discuss how to base systems on current business processes in later chapters.)

THIS IS THE TEAM'S BUSINESS PROCESS

This chapter emphasizes business process. The discussion would be incomplete if I didn't pass on a hard lesson I've learned: The focus needs to be on corporate business process, not that of only one individual. I've found it very easy to direct one key manager to define the business process, but the resulting perception does not represent the full reality of our business process.

For example, look again at my individual relationship with my PC. When I work on my PC, I control everything. I have my own way of thinking and interacting with my PC. In my head resides my understanding of how I have done things. My process is clear to me. Unfortunately, it is often totally unintelligible to those around me. My reality is not the reality of my associates.

American businesses are making a slow transition from individual focus to group or team focus. But individual managers are still assigned the job of defining and solving problems. Managers were taught to be in control. Isn't the manager the one who must have the answers? The manager acts alone to define the business process. *Mistake*!

Managers feel that if they're in charge, they must dictate the business system. The problem here is that the manager always has limited information. The manager doesn't understand fully all the necessary business requirements.

U.S. businesses have begun to attack the issue of individual versus team effort in product development. Ford designed the Taurus with a team consisting not just of product designers but of customers, manufacturers, suppliers, salespeople, service people, finance people, and others who had a stake in the total business process. As a result of this effort, the team developed and produced a car that had many advantages over previous Ford efforts. The Taurus was the top-selling car in the U.S. market. Ford's lesson in the product development area is that you need to involve all the participants in the process in order to obtain their ideas and to get them to buy into the team solution.

Many other businesses have learned the same lesson. Black & Decker, Boeing, and Federal Express are just a few of the many that have recognized that, to create the most desirable new products, all those involved in the business process must be part of the critical business process team. The lesson that we are learning is that everyone must be involved in the process for all aspects of the product. These aspects include design, manufacturing, delivery, and service of each new product to create the greatest market success.

EVERYONE GETS INVOLVED IN THE INFORMATION SYSTEM

The same holds true for the computer and communications technology that we utilize to create our internal information systems. Our businesses have become so complex that the only way to understand the full impact of the information systems that facilitate our business processes is to involve everyone in the process of selecting and implementing that information system technology.

It is only when this team development effort occurs that a business's full potential is realized. At that point an organization is fully able to understand the intricacies of its business process. Only with this understanding can we use technology and be sure that it enables the organization's "real" business process.

CONSIDER WHAT TECHNOLOGY CAN DO FOR YOUR ORGANIZATION

Technology can create a strategic advantage for an organization through advances in many areas and capabilities, such as:

- Customer service
- Ability to change quickly
- Customized products and services
- Getting your message to stakeholders
- Operations and overhead costs

The development of Web sites (internal sites and World Wide Web sites) makes an organization's information immediately available, in its most current form, to all those who have the need to know.

But as managers, we have to understand and develop this technology. We need to consider the following:

- Personal computers have gotten many of us involved without a strategy to allow our information to be useful to others who need it.

- Improvements in business processes must be the objective of the utilization of information technology.

- Everyone in the organization must be involved in how information technology is utilized.

CHAPTER 4

The On Time Project—It Can Be Done

by Bill Bysinger

"I do not need to write down my project plan—I have it all in my head."

"In this organization the project plans are a bother so we just have the secretary fill out the forms so that we keep the bureaucrats off our backs."

"We have a project schedule but no one believes it. We never get the projects completed on time."

"I tried using MicroSoft Project but it was a big waste of time."

"We started with a project plan but things changed so much that no one even looks at it now."

"Project plans are worthless!!!!"

When it comes to project plans, one of two things often happen. The technologists are not trained and therefore have no idea how to effectively utilize project planning tools or we, as managers, never participate or monitor the project planning process. In the first situation the technologists don't know how to do project planning and in the second they get the message from the managers that it is not of any value.

> Yes, we as managers have to take a major share of the responsibility in either situation.
>
> Bill presents a quick look at how to achieve ontime project delivery. As a manager who has often struggled with projects that continually are delayed I appreciate Bill's addressing this critical subject. One of the first steps in a manager's trust of technologists is to believe in their ability to deliver as promised. As a manager you want to have as few negative surprises as possible. Good project plans that are constantly monitored and updated eliminate surprises.
>
> Ken Knight

SCHEDULES MEAN BUSINESS CREDIBILITY

In the daily life of an Information Systems organization the key to being able to provide excellent customer service is good project management and ontime delivery of projects and technical support.

Traditionally MIS has been labeled as a group that never finishes anything on time. Most systems development projects are over budget and beyond schedule. In the business users minds this equates to non-accountability.

All other business organizations are held to high standards of objectives and delivery, but it appears MIS continues to make these a low priority.

Why is this the norm or the perceived norm of most information systems organizations?

It is not that MIS considers meeting objectives and making delivery dates less important, it's the demands placed on them to deliver too much too quick. This is due to an age old MIS projects problem, the phenomenon of scoping the size of a project and making clear, achievable estimates on projects.

MIS rarely demands project scope of their customers. They are too eager to please and rather than be honest about what is doable they underestimate the tasks required to do the job and over commit on the deliverables. Again, not because MIS is trying too fail, most often it is because they do not know how to say "No" gracefully.

This is the bane of the MIS existence. Most MIS people are pleasers, we hate to deliver "Bad" news. We try to evangelize the merits of what we will do for our customers, get them excited but then we disappointment them by not delivering ontime. This may be a generalization, but too often it becomes a self fulfilling prophesy.

There are only three areas in project management that really control delivery and quality.

SCOPE
TIME
RESOURCES

These are the determinants of whether you win or lose in the success of projects. Individually these three make up the life and effort devoted to project delivery.

1. Scope: This is the quantity of work that needs to be done, sometimes referred to as requirements, specifications, changes, functions, etc. These normally are comprised of things the users and managers of the functional organizations want you to deliver for them.

2. Time: This is the lapse time required to deliver the functions in finished form to the requesting/funding organization. This factor is usually dictated by the business unit requesting the work.

3. Resources: These are people, space, technology, training, tools, etc. needed to perform the work. These normally are difficult to acquire due to other commitments and funding available.

One way to look at these three factors is in terms of their ability to deliver value to the business. Do the requirements of this project deliver real value to the users? Do they create business opportunity or efficiency in the way we deliver products and services?

Is the investment in funding and rescue going to have a commensurate return.

Too often MIS will jump to the conclusion that what is needed is a good project management system. However, project management software does not necessarily make projects run faster or more cost efficient. In fact many times we spend more time on managing the project management system and not enough time managing the expectations of those requesting the project.

A methodology to manage a project coupled with a good project management software package can help the process. Again though this may only address the resource and time frame issue from a tracking perspective.

The real root cause of all late, over budget projects is more likely the "S" word, SCOPE.

Scope is many times the "root of all evil" in project management and execution.

If this is the problem, how do we get it under control?

A MODEL

At the beginning of every project, the process of gaining requirements and functionality needs to be managed with meticulous detail and the process of setting finite priorities and time frames is crucial. The following is one model for creating a better scope on projects.

1. Have the users (customers of the project) bring their wish list of features and functions to a meeting.

2. Rank order the wish list descending from those that represent the greatest need and greatest savings to those representing the least of these.

3. Check these lists with the users, who will be doing the work. The users who have input on these features and functions should be from the ranks of executives, managers, supervisors, and front line workers.

4. Set a number of acceptable requirements to build 50 percent to 70 percent of what is asked for to create the achieved project deliverable.

5. Prioritize this new list based on tangible advantages (dollar, efficiency, cost return) that would result in a feature or function being implemented.

6. Make an agreement that during the specification process, a second scoping can happen based on a prioritization, with consideration for scheduled delivery time.

7. Make the final scoping and proceed with the project.

8. Manage the users expectations throughout the project.

The above defined process delivers two things:

It allows for both the scope of the project and the resource constraints to be taken into account. These reinforce the ontime delivery of the project.

Now the question should be asked, what about the requirements that were scoped out of this project?

This is where versioning of applications software or MIS projects happens.

Assume for a minute that a normal development project takes 18 to 24 months from requirements through delivery into production. This should not be difficult to image since it continues to be the norm for many MIS organizations.

Why is this the case? Because we normally have too much to deliver and 18 months turns into 24 months or 36 months.

What if we took the 18 month project and said we will deliver it in six months?

How? By doing the two following things:

1. Limit scope based on doable ninety day development.
2. Version the project into three increments, with each being delivered on six month cycles, with six months in production before the next system comes online.

Why do it like this?

If you address the critical few, you will get the greatest return on process based on prioritization. Once the new technology is implemented, you will find out what the true next critical few should be.

In fact what you may find is that you are now able to deliver systems quicker and meet more schedules. The new business process you are supporting with the new applications and technology, create obsolescence in some of the normal requirements that would be addressed under the old model.

I have experienced good results with this type of model. The results have created faster project delivery and more satisfied customers.

AN EXAMPLE OF HOW IT WORKS

When I began to use this model, I was amazed at how it could impact the ability of my MIS organization to deliver ontime and on budget. At the same time the project fostered successful customer relationships with increased customer service.

My organization was asked to deliver a very large project on a six month schedule to be implemented by the following fiscal year. As I looked at the first cut features and functions list from the user department, I knew that we were in over our heads both in time commitment and resource commitment. Drastic measures had to be taken.

I called in my manager of systems development and said we needed to look at this project differently than any others. We needed to cut these requirements in half to deliver when expected and we had to get the user department deeply involved. We decided to build the former model.

1. We had a meeting with the users of the system and our development team in order to lay a plan for the project. In this meeting we defined the issue of scope and resources.

    There were too many features and functions to deliver in six months and we did not have the resources necessary to accomplish this project by the first of the year. However, we could deliver most of these features by the first of the year if MIS and the users could enter into a partnership on this project that would create success.

    (User Ownership became a paramount issue)

2. We assigned a user project manager (one of the user department managers) and an MIS project manager (my systems development manager). I signed up as the corporate executive sponsor and we had a meeting with the VP that the department reported to. This person became the project executive sponsor.

In the meeting we discussed the project process including the fact that we were not going to be able to deliver all the functionality requested but rather only the critical few. We would have to have a follow-up meeting to discuss projects delivered at later dates. This would address the functionality not delivered and new functionality uncovered as we brought this new system into production.

3. We then met with the users department representatives to go through a two day exercise in requirement scoping and requirement development. As part of this process we spent one day prior to the meeting observing the processes that needed to be changed as described in the request for the new system.

   In the meeting we had managers, supervisors, and front line workers. We started the meeting by asking the department manager to describe the processes we would be addressing. Then we asked the supervisor to either concur or change as appropriate. Finally we had the front line workers describe what they did in the processes.

   It was amazing how much variance there was between these three roles and their description of the process. It is no wonder that MIS has trouble delivering what the users really wants.

4. After settling and agreeing on the business processes, we mapped the process to look at the old and describe the new. From here, we started the process of requirements prioritization.

We took the features and functions list and defined requirements and quizzed the users on where the value from each of these would impact the business process.

I remember, in one instance a user asked for a specific capability and the supervisor was vehemently defending the need for this requirement to be high on the list.

I asked, "How much will this save you in process time a day or week?" The supervisor responded, "It will save my operators about 1 hour per day in total." I said, "Given the state of the current system and the changes and additions you want us to make in this new system, you are telling me this will save you about five hours per week or approximately 260 hours per year. On the MIS project side, this capability could take in excess of 150 hours of development time and take away from something that could be delivered in this same time that may have a greater impact." The pay back of her change was approximately $4,000 per year or .1 of one person (never a real recapture cost). In these terms she understood the reason this may not make the cut in high prioritized items.

After using this example, it became much clearer on the project team, not only how to prioritize, but that the sum total of the priorities would equal the total benefits and business advantages from the project.

5. By giving the users the input necessary to develop requirements for the project and helping them understand the nuances of development, they took true ownership in the project.

   (By the way, we also limited the amount of time we had to develop requirements and specifications to thirty days.)

6. After the list was prioritized, it was delivered to the design and development groups for estimating. Following these estimates, it was returned to the project requirements team to discuss what would fit into the now five month development and delivery into production schedule.

   The final prioritized list was looked over once more and it was decided that another version would come six to eight months after this version.

7. The end result was that the system was delivered on time, on budget, and the users felt a sense of ownership and customer satisfaction never before embodied in a project.

8. Finally, the following version was able to be developed with less of the functionality that was assumed but not developed in version 1.0.

THE BENEFITS

As I have explained in the example, if you follow this model both MIS and the customers of MIS benefit. You deliver more projects on schedule and you actually achieve a higher development to maintenance ratio. At the same time your customer satisfaction and acceptance of MIS as a strategic resource begins to become manifest in the business.

Remember the business is run on schedules and commitments and if you can prove that the difficult job of building, deploying, and implementing technology can deliver on time and on budget, your peers will support your efforts more vehemently.

Although this chapter has been a brief look at the schedule and project management, hopefully it has provided insight into a model that may work for you and your organization.

This has worked for me in many companies and with many Information System Organizations.

Trust me, this stuff works.

CHAPTER 5

Business Process Analysis—It Is Not Black Magic

by Ken Knight

"No one around here understands what the person next to them is doing."

"Everyone keeps tripping over each other. There just does not appear to be any order to the way we operate."

"You just do what you have to do! I do not have the slightest idea as to the limits of my responsibility."

"They ask me to design a computer system and I don't even know how we do things in that department"

In this chapter Ken discusses a key concept that occurs in any technology project; the analysis of the processes making up the business problem that will be improved through some form of technology implementation.

The basis for all quality management is good process work. This chapter deals with the implications of defining and understanding existing processes and redefining new processes. The steps taken and described in this chapter will lead to benefits and improvements in the way technology is delivered to the business.

The area of process can take an entire book to understand and define, we have taken a quick and easy approach to overview the need for business process analysis and some thoughts on how to do it.

Bill Bysinger

The key to business success continually changes. Today companies face multiple demands, rapid change, and strong competition. All of us find that the way our organizations operated in the past does not work today. Business process analysis has become one of our keys to survival. The business process analysis is a tool that helps us effectively promote change and innovation.

By utilizing business process analysis we have a tool that enables us to view current activities and procedures. We describe the activities and procedures involved and the information flows in and out of them. Once we are able to visualize our business processes we can then explore alternatives that may improve our performance.

Today, as a manager, I use business process analysis as a method for changing my organization's structure and current work flow. Business process analysis is a tool to determine how a potential technology investment can increase efficiency and make my organization more successful and profitable.

BUSINESS PROCESS ANALYSIS

A business process is the set of activities that represents the work and information flowing through an organization. Utilizing business process analysis represents a fundamental shift away from the functional/organizational view of business to one that focuses on how work flows through an organization. Launching a business process analysis project requires that the work and information flowing through your organization are well defined, clearly understood and accurately documented. The work and information flows should be clearly related to each of the business activities. There should also be a clear and supportable rationale for each activity which will then allow us to consider changes that might create improvements in performance.

I want to utilize business processes analysis to:

- improve the processes that add value for the company's customers
- eliminate the processes that do not add value for the company's customers

Examples of categories that can be selected for business process analysis include activities that:

- add value to their customers
- add no value to their customers
- cross several functional boundaries, creating bottlenecks and disconnects
- require significant organizational resources

- perform below expectations or perceived potential
- have inconsistent results, with fragmented accountability
- have required work, roles, and responsibilities that are not well defined and documented
- represent expensive technology solutions that have been acquired, but are not generating value to their customers

Business process analysis is a very practical method. It introduces a new way of thinking, merging business and information technology into a single activity. Instead of managers posing problems for technologists to solve by creating new applications, the two groups work together to create business process descriptions of the organization. These models provide a solid yet flexible structure on which alternative business solutions can be proposed and evaluated. Once a project team understands the existing process, new ways of doing business can be considered.

THE METHODOLOGY

The methodology provides a disciplined approach viewing work and information flows. Through a sequence of steps to be undertaken in a specific order. Applying these steps—Phases 1–5 on the following pages—reduces the risk of wasting time and expense, maximizes potential to develop a successful solution, defines completion, and provides clear deliverables with near-term payoff by enhancing clarity and understanding of the business activity.

Phase 1: Analyze the Business Environment and Capture The Processes That Need to Be Mapped

The actual analysis phase begins when high level macro processes are identified. In most organizations, the macro processes will be extremely complex and large. Therefore, they need to be broken down into the smaller and more manageable detailed micro processes. Detailed micro processes will be the ones that will be illustrated and captured in our data flow charts. During this phase we define processes to be analyzed. First we create a project plan and schedule of deliverables. It is critical that we understand the business processes and scope to be analyzed.

Let us consider a simple example. An insurance company has as one of its primary business processes the processing of their insured loss claims. In this case we define the macro process as the major activities of the company's claim activity. The project deliverable will be a mapping of the work flows through the claims activity from the reported loss to an agent to the insured receipt of their insurance check. Figure 5-1 shows this flow.

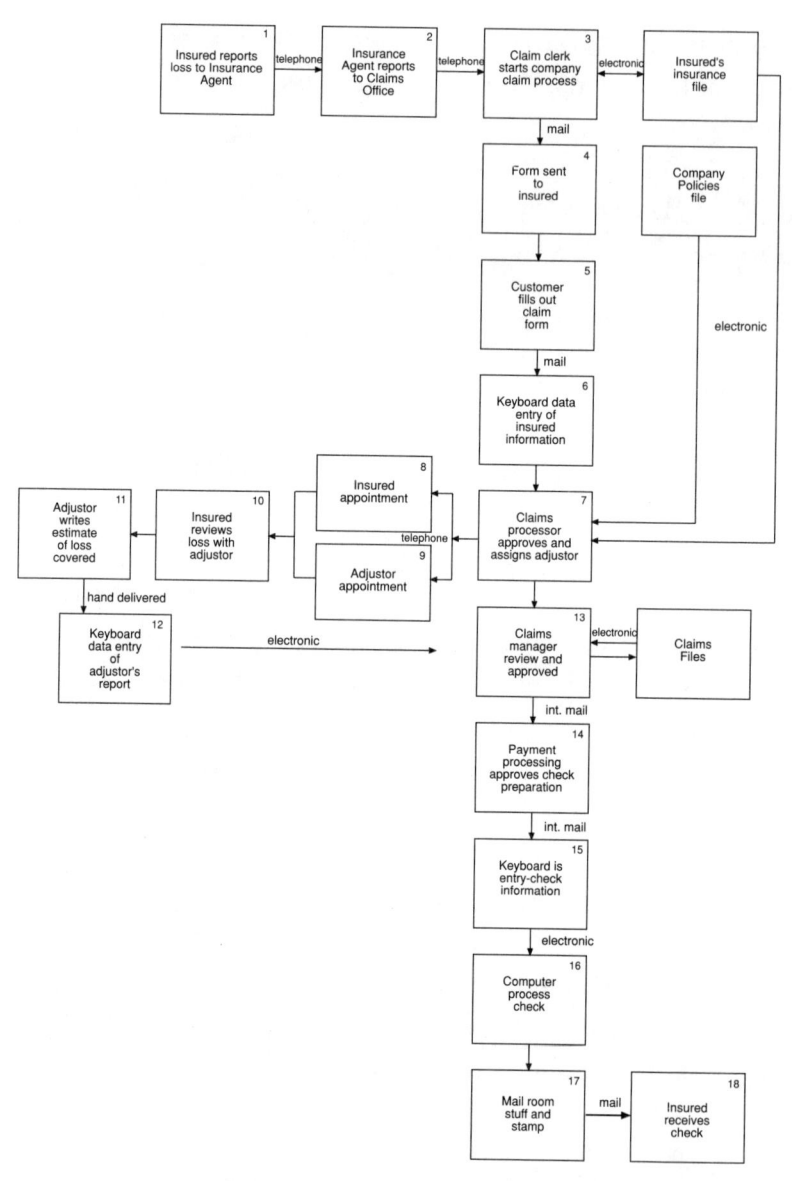

Figure 5-1 Insurance Claim Process.

For each of the work activities there are likely micro processes that we will also want to define. In our insurance claim example let us look at the single process activity labeled claim clerk starts company claim process (box 3 in Figure 5-1). Figure 5-2 presents the further detailed specification of this process.

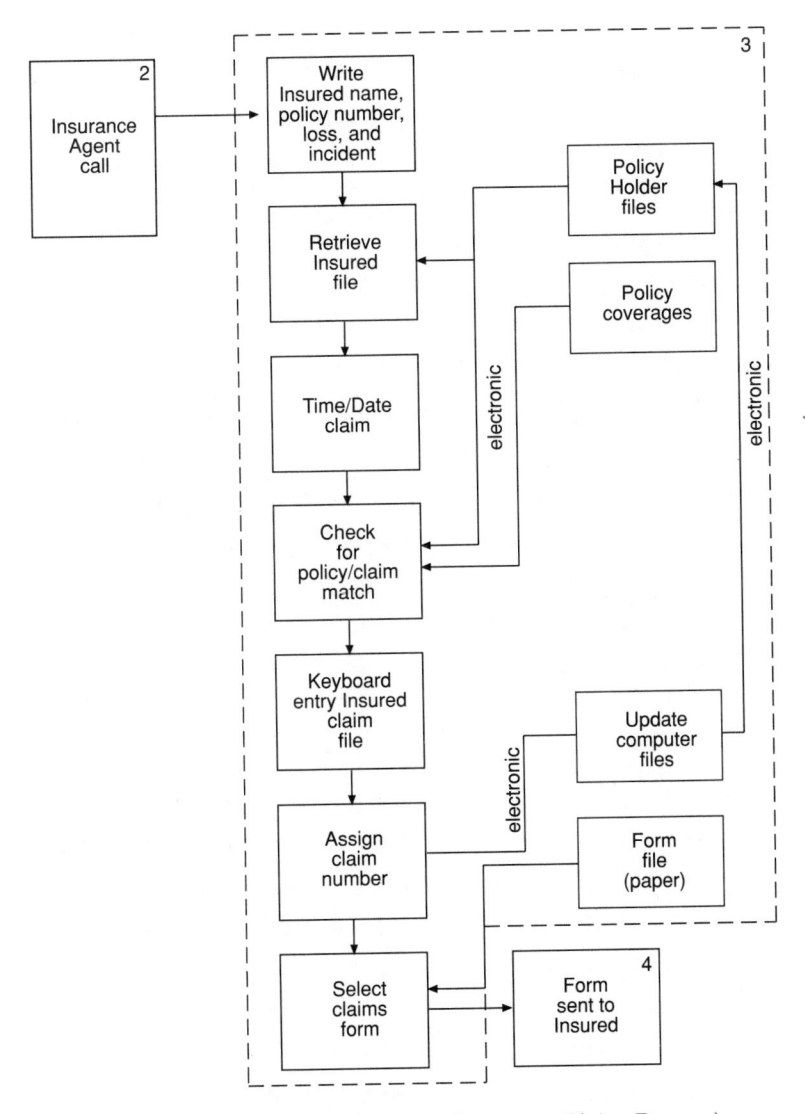

Figure 5-2 Claim Clerk (Start Company Claim Process).

Phase 2: Capture the Current "As-Is" Situation—Process Mapping

Capture the current work flow exactly as it is along with its micro processes if needed. Process mapping is at the heart of business process analysis. Start with a mapping session with the process owners. These are the people who do the work and who are most knowledgeable about the actual work flow.

Employees usually lack formal tools and techniques for visualizing work flows. In order to develop their work and make the processes more structured and less complicated, process mapping is required.

Process mapping captures work and charts information flows to illustrate the process and its steps. During the process mapping, flow charts are recorded with all available additional information related to the business process simultaneously collected. These additional items may include existing forms, tally sheets, reports, instruction and operations manuals.

Process mapping is a way to illustrate "as-is" and "could be" views of processes. By visualizing work flows, process mapping promotes effective communication between team members, customers, managers, and others.

Process maps present the work flow path of data, roles, and responsibilities in the organization's operations. The "as-is" represents the current work flows. These contain the existing business rules, activities, information, sequence of activities, functional responsibilities, activity ownership, information utilized or generated, and so forth.

The mapping is done in sufficient detail to be clearly read by all those who are involved in the business process analysis project.

The process maps define the steps involved in the business process. Process map displays are so simple to create that even novices can draw them. These maps display the processes that take one or more input and create output that has value to a customer. That customer may be someone within the organization or an external individual or organization.

Process mapping is important because these maps can capture all the useful and related information such as open issues, unclear processes, and micro processes. Where there is a micro process, yet another process exists inside that process. Another layer of the organizations activity needs to be studied and a process map generated.

Once the initial process map is generated, review the first version with the process owners/executors to verify the content and accuracy. At that time, modify as required.

In Figures 5-1 and 5-2 we have shown two examples of the "as-is" for our insurance claim process.

This process mapping tool/methodology provides a disciplined approach and specific methods for seeing how the organization is functioning. Process mapping reduces the risk of miscommunication, maximizes potential to develop alternative solutions, defines completion of the "as-is" analysis, and provides clear deliverables.

Phase 3: Analyze the "As-Is" and Develop a Vision of the "Could-be" Solution

Analyze Phase 2 findings. Determine if a revision in the process might be helpful. Key issues:

- What are the primary micro processes, activities, and steps that constitute our selected business activity?
- In what order are these micro processes performed?
- How do resources, information, and work flow through each of the micro processes?
- Why is the work performed as it is?
- What assumptions are done about the current work flow, policies, and procedures?
- What are the key strengths and weaknesses of each selected micro process or the entire macro process?

Consider the boundaries between "our" own processes and those of business partners e.g., customers (internal and external), suppliers, strategic allies, etc..

- How could these boundaries be redefined in order to improve overall performance?
- What are the specific improvement goals for the modified processes?

For example, in our claims processing example in Figure 5-1, could the insurance company eliminate some of the steps in the claims process? Let's consider that now.

In this phase (box 3 in Figure 5-1) we consider whether movement of steps among activities, activities among processes, or reassigned responsibility for steps will improve performance. We also identify instances in which better coordination among activities would improve performance. Rethink activities whenever possible to eliminate separate micro processes. Resequence activities and minimizing the number and complexity of micro processes. Reduce the number and complexity of steps, and place activities in a more logical order to facilitate flow.

For example: Let's look at our processes displayed in Figures 5-1 and 5-2. There are ways that we could simplify the process. First by eliminating some of the individuals involved in the process including the claims processor and the claims manager; then we could have the information directly entered into the computer by the person generating it. In Figure 5-3 we redesign the whole process from the initial 18 steps macro-process to a new 5 step macro process. This is accomplished by the initial claims representative setting up an appointment between the insured and the adjuster. The adjuster in this new process has a greatly expanded roll. She gathers all the detail loss information from the insured, enters it into the computer, has access to all the insurance company relevant files (Insured insurance file, Company polices files, and Claims files), makes a loss decision, gets the insured's approval, and writes a check to the insured on the spot.

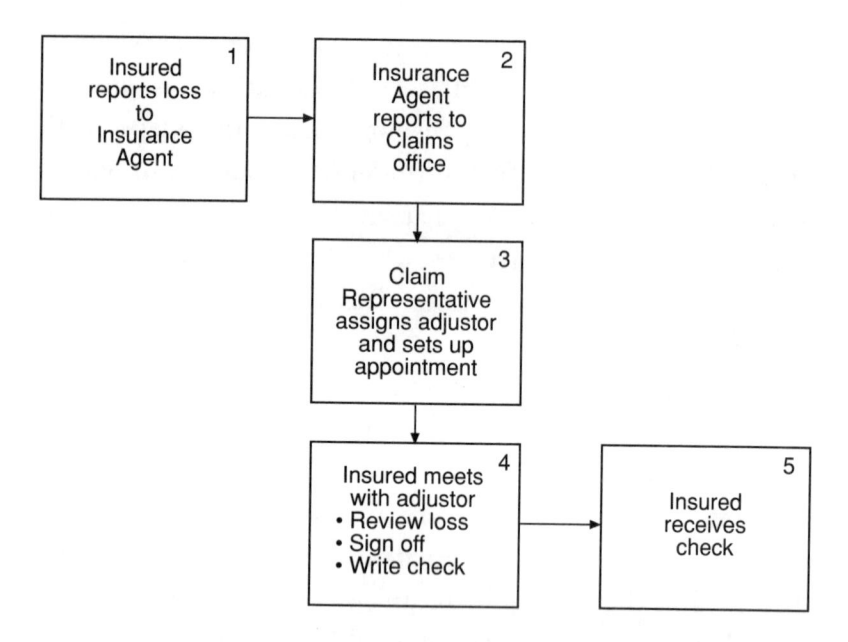

```
┌─────────────┐ 1   ┌─────────────┐ 2
│  Insured    │     │  Insurance  │
│ reports loss│────▶│    Agent    │
│     to      │     │ reports to  │
│  Insurance  │     │   Claims    │
│    Agent    │     │    office   │
└─────────────┘     └──────┬──────┘
                           │
                           ▼
                    ┌─────────────┐ 3
                    │    Claim    │
                    │Representative│
                    │assigns adjustor│
                    │ and sets up │
                    │ appointment │
                    └──────┬──────┘
                           │
                           ▼
        ┌──────────────────┐ 4   ┌──────────┐ 5
        │ Insured meets    │     │ Insured  │
        │ with adjustor    │────▶│ receives │
        │ • Review loss    │     │  check   │
        │ • Sign off       │     │          │
        │ • Write check    │     │          │
        └──────────────────┘     └──────────┘
```

Figure 5-3 Redefined Insurance Claim Process.

In one insurance company I saw the claims processing cost was reduced by over 70 percent and the average time to process a claim ranged from four working days to three weeks.

The 70 percent drop in claims processing cost was great for the company's profits. The decrease in claims processing time created very satisfied and loyal customers. The company now would like to bring the time to process the claim down to an average of two working days.

Phase 4: Define The Individual Roles and Responsibilities for the "As-Is" or "Could-be" Process Map.

Model the roles of those who perform the work now. For the "could-be" map detect the current habits or patterns of behavior that need to be altered in order to accommodate the newly designed solution. Determine which resources will need training and re-tooling. Model the roles to support the newly envisioned, future designed work flow.

- What are the roles and responsibilities?
- Who will be responsible for which activities?
- What are the priorities and dependencies?
- What goals and targets should be established?
- Will roles and responsibilities change?
- If so, how? What training will be needed?
- What will the new organization look like?

In Figure 5-4 we display a different process—Purchase Order Process. In this figure the individuals who will perform each function, roles and responsibilities, are shown in ( ) at the top of each box.

Here we might decide to simplify the process with a new "could-be" process map by increasing the authority of each employee and go directly form box 2 in Figure 5-4 to box 8. This would eliminate steps 3, 4, 5, 6 & 7 in the "as-is" Purchase Order Process.

70 Investing in Information Technology

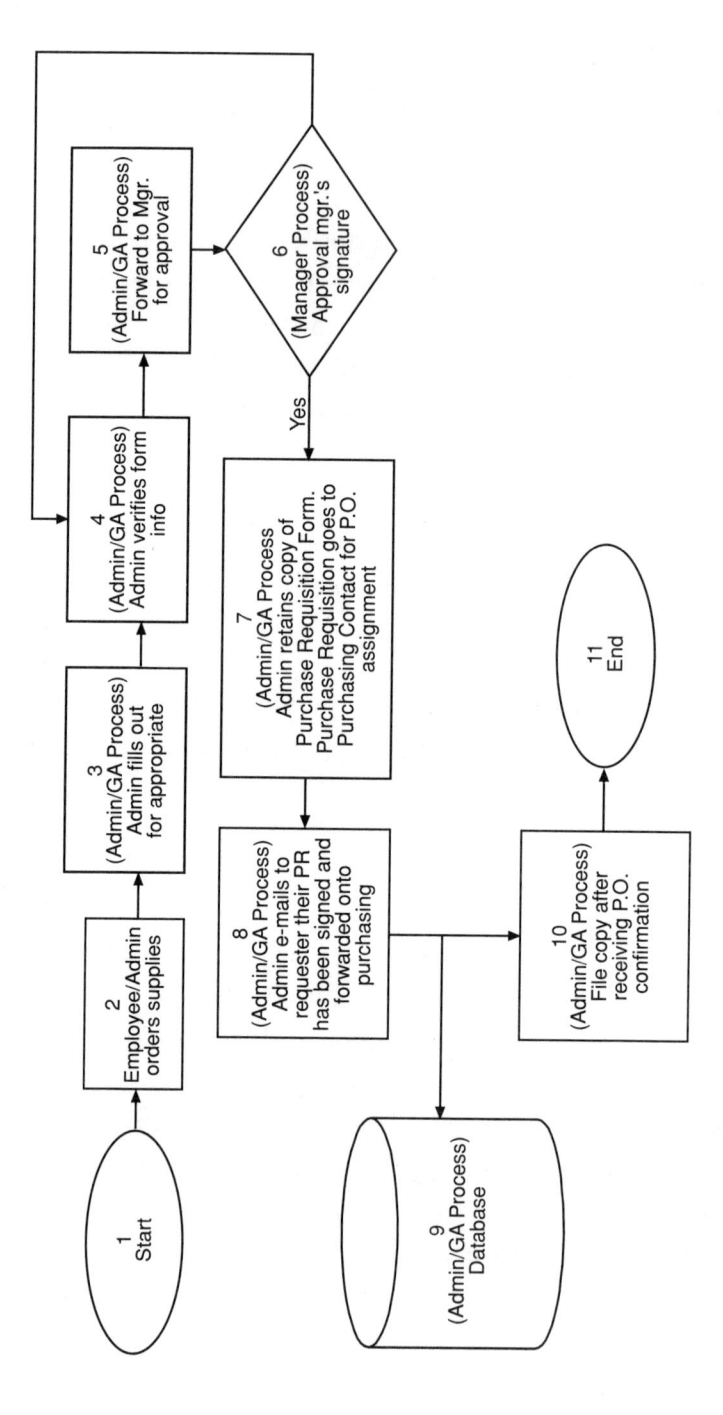

Figure 5-4 Purchase Order Process.

1. Start
2. (Employee/Admin) orders supplies
3. (Admin/GA Process) Admin fills out appropriate
4. (Admin/GA Process) Admin verifies form info
5. (Admin/GA Process) Forward to Mgr. for approval
6. (Manager Process) Approval mgr.'s signature
7. (Admin/GA Process) Admin retains copy of Purchase Requisition Form. Purchase Requisition goes to Purchasing Contact for P.O. assignment
8. (Admin/GA Process) Admin e-mails to requester their PR has been signed and forwarded onto purchasing
9. (Admin/GA Process) Database
10. (Admin/GA Process) File copy after receiving P.O. confirmation
11. End

Phase 5: Project Delivery Review and Analysis

Once a project is completed, deliver it to all those who need to be informed.

Analyze how well the business process has been mapped in both the "as-is" and "could-be" analysis. The review and analysis needs to be part of every project and should represent the organization's continual process improvement culture. This will be a primary focus of Chapter 7.

SUMMARY

Every company strives to improve. But before processes can be improved, it must be made clear exactly what the current ones are. This is the primary benefit of business process analysis. It forces people to recognize that there are existing work flows they are following even though they had not previously been written down. Once they reorganize this, they can work on changing the work flow process from an "as-is" state toward a "could-be."

CHAPTER 6

The Challenge: Communicating in Business Terms

by Bill Bysinger

"Do you want to use OS/2 Warp, NT 3.51, SC Unix or Zenix?"

"ISDN will solve all your problems!"

"Your new PC has a 16MB EDO ECC DIMM RAM."

"We should switch to CD-ROM (with SCSI II port) to load NT."

"We will need to install more routers in Chicago"

Technologists, please talk to me in my language!!

Bill squarely addresses the above issue in this chapter. As a manager I am tired of "techno speak". Being able to talk in a jargon the manager does not understand may make you feel more valuable, but it does not help me. In fact, it makes me suspicious of you and your motives. Tell it to me so that I can clearly understand, in language that I use. Thanks Bill! I needed this.

Ken Knight

When dialogue on business process begins between IS managers and business managers, we encounter a problem. Information systems people, especially IS managers, need to be able to communicate effectively with businesspeople. I don't mean to say that IS people need to go to business school, but they need to stop using three-letter acronyms to describe everything.

Having been in the technology business for over twenty-five years, it interests me to hear terms like RAM, CPU, MB, and LAN used by mainstream people on the radio and television and in print. Whenever possible, I resist using these terms in discussions of the business need of a customer. In fact, I would rather discuss how I can solve a problem from a business perspective than discuss hardware or network technology.

SPEAK IN BUSINESS LANGUAGE

I have a friend who is also a senior IS executive. He told me that he believes his effectiveness is based on listening to customers. By communicating in their terms, he offers feedback and explains to them the ways in which he can be of assistance. In all my assignments as the senior executive in IS organizations, I have found that I am most effective when I can speak the language of the business.

I believe that much of the success of my efforts in IS begins with the ability to communicate in simple terms. I summarize my value–added in simple models that fit on one 8-1/2-by-11-inch sheet of paper. On each one, I explain my directions, information system's architecture, objectives, and mission in easy-to-understand terms.

When I assume responsibility for an IS organization, one of the first tasks I take on is to determine our mission and objectives. Once these are defined, I publish them throughout the company for all to see. Defining mission and objectives may seem like a distraction from our real work but in reality, it can be quite helpful. I've consulted for over fifty significant firms and, during this time, I've found less than 10 percent with clearly articulated, measurable missions and related objectives. And though most of the missions and objectives sound nice, they're not tangible enough to make a difference.

Over the past twenty-five years, I've built six technology-based organizations from my senior executive position. For each company, I made sure that IS had a clearly defined, measurable mission and a set of objectives that mirrored the objectives of the business. Since measurement must be defined in business terms, I don't know how a technology organization can function without these or how it can measure its success.

Define Mission

The IS mission transcends time. It should reflect an ongoing commitment to the business. For example, a mission statement that reads: "IS will provide systems to enhance the business," is far too vague. If, on the other hand, it reads: "The mission of IS is to provide systems that increase global communications, provide timely financial information, promote increased profitability, and deliver efficiency to reduce operational costs," the statement is useful, measurable through annual objectives, and not too technical for everyone to understand.

Define Objectives

The IS objectives should be annualized and measurable for performance monitoring.

How about this objective: "IS will extend the global network to encompass LANs." *Wrong*! It says how you'll do "it" but doesn't say what "it" is. Instead try: "Information systems will supply a communications capability to provide daily communication of sales information to all regions worldwide." This is a good objective because it says what you plan to accomplish in a way that allows you to measure your accomplishment.

Everything that the business asks IS to do should tie in with an objective that supports the IS mission. And the IS mission and objectives should support the sum total of the company's mission and objectives.

While IS makes the transition to become a more focused organization funded by the business process, it becomes critical that IS be able to articulate the reasons for its existence and do so clearly to anyone in the business. I also believe that anyone in my organization should be able to articulate the IS mission and objectives in presentations to new employees during orientations or to internal customers who ask what we do.

I recall one day when a new division director stopped me in the hall and asked if IS could build a system for him that he could not live without. And, if we could, would I be committed to the system?

My response was, "Is this an objective that's in your budget for this fiscal year?"

He answered, "No, but my people tell me we really need it to do our work."

I replied, "Maybe we could determine how it could be funded by the business. We should discuss this with the COO."

He was surprised that I suggested a business funding discussion. "I thought your job was to solve my problems."

I told him that it was my job to solve problems for people through better use of technology. However, I was also a financial steward of the company and, therefore, needed to determine funding sources prior to taking on any project.

I've played my part in this same scene in many companies. Pointing to the funding question has given me high credibility in my management of the financial aspects of IS. This emphasis also enables the company to get a better picture of how technology resources are being spent.

Remember as a technology manager, you're a business person first and a technologist second. Too often, we forget this. Our tendency is to jump to a technology solution before examining the ramifications of our actions for the business.

Business Terms

Businesspeople bat around words that are foreign to IS managers and make them uncomfortable. Several examples follow.

- *Profitability*: An important concept since every IS dollar is normally allocated or is measured against some form of future results.

- *Funding (budget)*: IS uses the company's money to provide something in return and to enable others.

- *Market*: IS should provide opportunities to enter new markets or to increase existing ones.

- *Return on investment*: IS should provide measurability and substantiation of the return on investment.

- *Value*: Every dollar spent on technology should have a corresponding value since all dollars should be used to advance the business or provide more company resources.

- *Performance*: IS must provide the company with measurements to judge not only the performance of IS but all aspects of the business.

- *Industry-specific*: As Steve Ballmer of Microsoft says, "We should eat our own dog food." It is important to use what you sell. The company's technology must be enabled to help the company respond better to the market. Information systems must understand clearly the market needs of the industry you provide products or services to.

Some Companies That Deliver

I have always looked to companies that have been good at delivering something as models for how I should deliver systems to the corporation. Some model companies are:

- *Lands' End*: Lands' End must have one of the best order-processing systems in the catalog business. Every time I call them, they treat me like a friend. They not only know what I have bought from them in the past, they make suggestions about other merchandise I may find interesting. After they ask me how I want my order shipped, they guarantee delivery.

- *Nordstrom*: They clearly understand customer service. Nordstrom also allows cross-selling to make sure that the customer is well taken care of. Company policy is to cater to customer need.

- *Hallmark*: I assume that their quality-control and distribution systems must be efficient, because I always see full shelves in their stores. Hallmark stays in tune with the market by offering high-quality merchandise.

- *NEXT Computer*: Although they are out of the hardware business, their manufacturing systems are evidence of an astoundingly simple and efficient application of technology.

I believe that good models for systems applications are extremely helpful. Such real-life examples can help your company understand how to improve in certain operational areas, perhaps by observing better models than the ones that exist in your current industry.

MY MISSION

I see my mission as empowering the business through technology by applying technology to enable existing and new business processes. If I do this right and communicate it well to the company, I don't have to worry about my relevance to the business.

BUSINESS COMMUNICATION TOOLS

INFORMATION SYSTEMS MANAGERS:

1. Always deliver results that are measurable and reportable.
2. Use business terms to describe results and measurements.
3. Build a mission statement that reflects what the business needs.
4. Base all annual objectives on "key" business objectives.
5. Tie all results of IS back to the business objectives.
6. Report monthly on how IS is tracking on the business objectives.

Examples of Results Reporting

Technology availability: Use a bar graph of available time versus up-time and compare to manufacturing productivity.

Fiscal Responsibility

Pie chart percentage of budget measurements of actual versus results delivered by IS during most recent fiscal period (examples: projects delivered on time, new technologies implemented, users trained in systems, remote offices supported, number of users on the systems, inventory of processors and software packages supported per user).

Business Value

Through a bar chart, show projects by phases.

Examples:

Requirements definition	20%
Design	20%
Coding	30%
Testing	10%
Configuring	5%
Training	5%
Implementing	10% (initial users only)

Sample: Client/server time horizon as a percentage of total project.

Human Resources

Staff percentage dedicated to supporting existing systems and technologies versus those dedicated to new systems and to bringing new technologies to the business.

Target should be 30 percent in support and 70 percent in developing and implementing new technologies for the business.

The art of reporting in business terms is critical to creating and exposing the value information systems brings to the business.

This report should be delivered to all business managers as an information systems value bulletin monthly, and the more graphic the better.

CHAPTER 7

How to Implement Technology: Managing for Continual Improvement

by Ken Knight

"In MIS we live with process every day. We are structure driven and we live by procedures and policies. It seems like when we begin a project, the users never understand the need for discipline. It is more about how long will this take and how much is it going to cost."

"The larger the project the more pressure and many times the less discipline we have. In fact in some projects there is excitement on the front end, but the longer we are at it the less the user groups want to be involved."

"I remember when we put in the new sales system it was like no one had time to participate, they didn't like the project structure and they resisted in making the project task commitments."

Process is critical for systems and even more crucial for business systems projects. It is the make or break scenario. Understanding and commitment is necessary for business and MIS to work together to gain quality.

In Chapter 7 Ken emphasizes the key importance of having a process to deliver systems successfully into the business. He concentrates on the components of the process that ensure good business information assessment, good

> *project management, resource allocation, measurement, and quality. These are the business tenants that must be shared by both the information systems professionals and the business users. Ken is very clear in both process and examples of why this is a key element of successful systems delivery.*
>
> **Bill Bysinger**

We've discussed understanding our business process and defining our mission as preconditions for developing systems that actually enable business processes. Now, let's look at how to implement systems most effectively.

Part of "making it simple" in IS is having a structured way to go about implementing computer and information systems technology. To do this, I'll develop a methodology based on several well-defined management techniques. If I'm developing information systems that enhance my business processes, my organization will become more effective and efficient. My firm can become more competitive in the eyes of my customers, which is a necessity for firms in highly competitive businesses.

The best feature of this methodology is its clearly defined steps. Such clear steps help me frame exactly how and what will be done. And these steps are easy to communicate to everyone in my organization. They help to avoid a situation I find myself in all too often: a manager struggling with a grandiose technology scheme—what I call "a pie-in-the-sky proposal." It is typical of this scenario that utilization of new technology is poorly defined, supported only by a blind belief that it will solve all the organization's problems. Watch out for pies in the sky—you usually end up eating air!

THE RUSH TO CLIENT/SERVER TECHNOLOGY

One example of a pie-in-the-sky is distributed-network, client/server technology. I often hear client/server touted as the solution for all problems. But, in almost every case, I have seen implementation create great confusion and, in some situations, nightmares. I have seen costs escalate, data structures become confused, security disappear, and chaos reign.

Faculty at the Seattle Pacific University School of Business and Economics work with two of the largest network users in the United States. Both are large public corporations. One is a young hi-tech firm producing key components that make networks function. The second is a large manufacturing firm that is committed to moving away from a centralized mainframe computing environment and toward distributed computing with a PC on every desk.

Both organizations are trying to make distributed client/server networked technology the basis of their mission-critical information systems. In both cases, the organization does not have clear plans as to how they are going to implement this technology. Both organizations suffer from great confusion in their efforts to implement new mission-critical technology. Both could benefit from the implementation methodology proposed here.

Again, mission-critical information systems include required functions like production, sales, accounting, payroll, and customer service. If a mission-critical system goes down for even a few hours, the firm's performance of productive activities comes to a screeching halt.

In my earlier example, when Southwest Airlines' reservation and ticketing system went down, it was a good example of a mission-critical system failing. The growing line of irate customers indicated that, if Southwest's system stayed down for a few hours, the airline would have many more angry customers and financial losses. Eventually, employees would have scrambled frantically to ticket the passengers with a makeshift manual system just to move them onto airplanes.

This example from Data Communications' *"Tales from the Crypt"* shows how one company spent an additional $484,000 to clean up a mess created by a $150,000 purchase.

TALES FROM THE CRYPT
By Daniel M. Gasparro, Contributing Editor

Here's another horror story from a large company whose budget is decided behind closed doors in the boardroom. Each year the board looks at profits, decides what new markets to enter, determines how much it would cost to penetrate the targets (not counting networking/IT), and assesses its exit rate (the amount spent on capital acquisition and general expenses that year). At that point it arrives at a lump sum (whatever was left over that didn't have a negative impact on the bottom line) and gives it to the networking/IT department.

It was up to the technology folks at this world-class outfit to look appropriately grateful and try to keep the network going on what they were given. Just to make sure that disaster was imminent, the board members and the networking/IT staff never discussed what tools were needed to meet company goals.

Into this gap flew the sales machine from Microsoft Corp. (Redmond, Wash.). It talked upper management into a network operating system, desktop-and LAN-based productivity applications, and corporate-wide e-mail—all for the bargain price of $150,000.

It wasn't long after installation and configuration began that the network started to sag under the weight of the new applications. It turns out the existing infrastructure was pretty creaky, and loading on the latest applications revealed hidden problems. There was no segmentation strategy on any of the LANs. Instead of being planned the network evolved, with users being added willy-nilly to servers and segments. The WAN circuits—64-kbit/s leased lines—were deliberately under-engineered to save money.

Things got really ugly when the LAN applications collided with the Unix programs and other software already up and running. Microsoft's protocols of choice at that point were Netbios and Netbeui. Both are unroutable, broadcast-oriented mechanisms that waste huge amounts of WAN bandwidth. Since the company's network was mainly bridged, broadcast storms and black holes were the order of the day. Then, in a misguided attempt to save money, the firm insisted that users access a central application repository over the WAN, without setting proper-use policies. WAN bandwidth, already stretched thin, snapped under the strain, and the network suffered severe outages. Inside estimates suggest that every time the network went down—and it was almost a regular occurrence—it cost plenty in wasted productivity.

Fixing the problem required routers, hubs, and cabling to properly segment users and departmental traffic. That cost roughly $400,000. WAN bandwidth was first jumped to TI (1.544 Mbit/s); later, it was taken much higher—for $84,000 a year. The almost $500,000 spent cleaning up the mess dwarfs the $150,000 top management expected to pay. Here again, the total doesn't include lost productivity.

To make matters worse, top management blamed networking/IT for the cost overruns. Clearly, the lack of any meaningful dialogue had a devastating effect on business. Corporate networkers understand that the infrastructure is multilayered and complex. They've got to be able to communicate this to top management. Unfortunately, corporados tend to think that adding new applications is pretty much a matter of tearing the shrink-wrap.

Source: *Data Communications;* October 1995, pages 61–62.

THE METHODOLOGY

My methodology is based on a traditional project management framework. The methodology is displayed in Figure 7.1.

Step 1

Step 1 creates a project culture which, in turn, generates a culture of open communication and teaming of all participants. The project culture continues through every step of this implementation methodology.

```
                    CREATE A
                    PROJECT
                    CULTURE
                   ↗        ↖
    COMMUNICATE              DESCRIBE AND
    COMMUNICATE              DISPLAY THE
    COMMUNICATE              DESIRED
                             BUSINESS
                             PROCESS
         ↑                        ↓
    EVALUATE—                DEVELOP THE
    A CONTINUOUS             TECHNICAL
    IMPROVEMENT              SCOPE
    PROCESS                  —technical evaluation
                             —financial evaluation
         ↑                        ↓
    MODIFY THE
    SYSTEM TO
    ACHIEVE
    ACCEPTABLE  ←            INTRODUCE THE
    TECHNICAL AND            PROTOTYPE
    BUSINESS
    OBJECTIVES
```

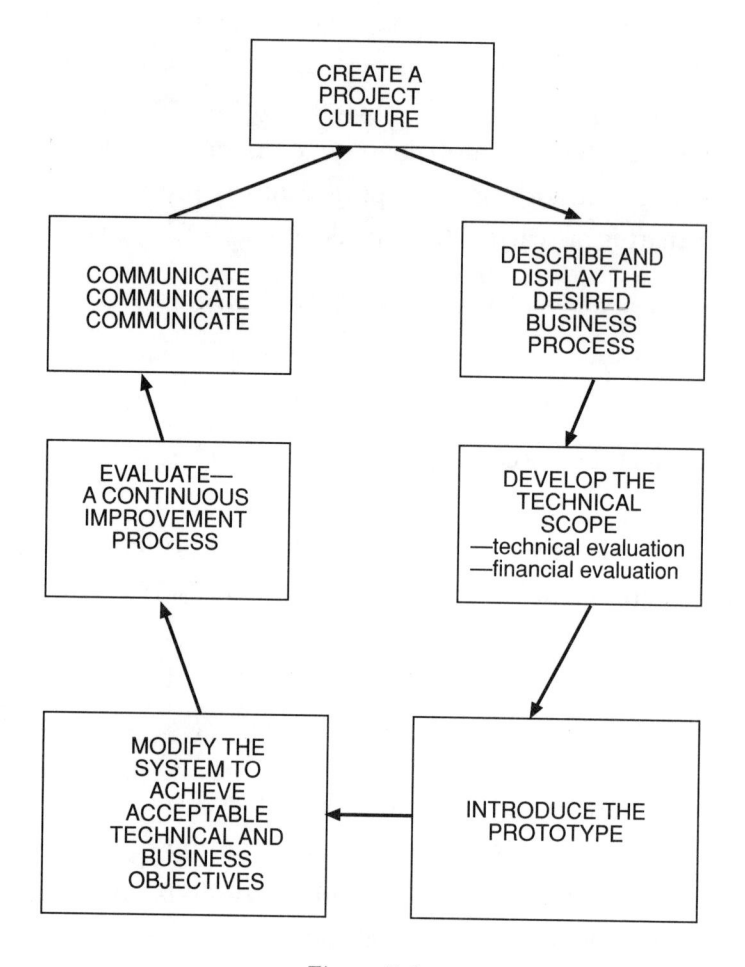

Figure 7.1

Step 2

Step 2 develops a clear description of the business process. At this point, not only is the process described but it is understood by all interested and involved parties, each of whom has also to understand the business process as it is viewed by the others. As understanding is shared, a more accurate scope of the business process evolves. The objective of Step 2 is to define the desired business process.

Step 3

Step 3 limits the scope of the technology implementation, describes the scope, and reaches consensus on the proposed changes. It is important to analyze and develop project feasibility from both technical and business perspectives.

Step 4

Step 4 then implements the agreed-upon, limited improvement using a prototype. Putting a prototype system in users' hands produces quick feedback on what the system can actually accomplish, so that it can be determined if the new technology enhances the business process as expected.

Step 5

Step 5 modifies the prototype as the system becomes operational. Learn and adapt quickly to achieve the project's technical and business objectives.

Step 6

Step 6 begins when full implementation has been completed. In this step, the continuous improvement process is set in motion. This starts with an open and honest evaluation of the business and technical accomplishments.

Step 7

Step 7 of the methodology reemphasizes Step 1. The project team continually emphasizes communication. One thing to remember here: Keep the lines open for bad news as well as good and, if it's bad, don't kill the messenger.

In order to more completely understand how these steps are involved in the methodology of traditional project management, let us take a closer look:

Step 1: Project Culture of Communication and Teaming

I see an ever-increasing degree of specialization in organizations today. Because knowledge is advancing rapidly, I am ever more aware that I need to hire people who have far more knowledge about their jobs than I do. Early in my career, hiring smarter and more knowledgeable people was not an easy thing for me. I am a typical type-A person; I like to be in control at all times. After all, my job as manager is to know everything about my business, isn't it? But my people have information and knowledge that I don't possess—knowledge that's essential in our complex business process. As our business process changes further, I have no choice but to rely on those around me.

Create a Project Team

Our goal in this first step is to establish a project team to develop and document a team understanding of our business process. It is important at the outset to obtain quality representation from all key constituents. A constituent is anyone who will give input to the project or will be impacted by the project. Here, quality representation is important, meaning that the project team should be seen as a high-status assignment. Only the best people are chosen for the team. The last thing that anyone wants is a team that views the project as a tour in Siberia or a second-class assignment for second-class people.

The project team's objective is to utilize new computer and communication technology to improve the business process. The team needs to see its task as important. Make it clear that each team member has the potential to create significant good for both the company's and his or her own benefit. In this positive environment, each member must see that all members have contributions to make. While the business process manager is the team coordinator, all have critical inputs that will be needed to generate a successful project outcome.

Facilitate Team Communication

Once a project team is selected, each member must learn to communicate with the others on the team. Effective communication doesn't just happen in teams, most often because of two significant barriers. The first is the hierarchy that exists in any organization. People whose organizational unit is perceived as lower or whose individual status in the company is lower have a difficult time either speaking up without being asked or challenging those who out rank them, even when they know that the superior is wrong.

The second barrier to communication is jargon. As we pursue our own discipline or work tasks, we develop the language of our discipline or work group. Such jargon is a shorthand that facilitates communication in our work team. Unfortunately, the multiplicity of such special languages produces words or phrases that are often defined differently by each functional area of our organization. For example, "system" means computer hardware or software to an IS manager. To the business manager, the same term refers to a business process system, that is a set of tasks.

Producing effective communication in the team requires a concerted effort by everyone on the team. This effort begins with listening skills. Expository skills come second. When the team progresses in its ability to communicate, each member comes to feel understood. A member who feels understood feels like a part of the team. By fostering communication, the manager is generating a culture that encourages cooperation and support.

Step 2: Business Process Description

The business process must be described so that it is understood by the project team. Often, however, the term *busi-*

ness process is used without being understood.

The business process consists of the flow of work, information, and physical product through the organization. A short description of the business process gives the project team a systems description of how the business operates. The description covers the tasks performed on information or physical product, specifies who performs the tasks, and traces the orderly flow of tasks through the organization.

Business processes usually cross several functional lines in an organization. The big picture, crossover nature of the business process can make it difficult for a team to visualize without being provided with a good definition.

If we take a quick look at a company that builds and sells custom furniture, we might find that the business process flows as follows: Sales acquires the customer; manufacturing builds the furniture to order; shipping delivers the finished furniture; finance collects payment from the customer; accounting records the completed transaction; and customer service provides the follow-up service and maintenance on the furniture. Clearly, throughout the business process, many different tasks are performed by employees in the different functional areas of the organization.

The objective in this step is to establish the desired business process. Creativity counts and is valued. This is a time to rethink what the organization does and how it carries out its business and then to describe the desired business process, which is the desired flow of work, materials, and information to accomplish the organization's business objectives.

Step 3: Project Scope for Rapid Completion and Realized Return

In today's business environment, projects that take several years to complete are often obsolete before they are functional. Let me explain what I mean by "obsolete." When the business process changes, the implemented system models the old business process, which is no longer operational. The system is thus rendered obsolete. It no longer has a purpose.

I've learned a lesson from listening to my information systems managers over the years: Changes in my high-technology computer and communications systems need to be limited in scope. A rule of thumb applicable to most organizations is that almost any technology information systems project undertaken should have a completion time line of no more than 90 or 120 days. The era in which the computer group has a two- or four-year backlog should be long gone.

The key is to select projects that can be accomplished within the 90- to 120-day target period. If projects on the current "to-do" list are all of longer duration, cancel them. Go back and work with the process managers. Determine where they see opportunities for using technology to enable improvement in the business process. The key question here is how a technology can be used quickly to enable the desired business process.

The project team sets the scope of the project. The information systems manager is responsible for accomplishing the project within the proposed budget and time frame. Projects selected will be ones that the business process manager can assure will create value. In the next chapter, we will discuss in detail the process by which the organization achieves value from its technology investments.

Develop a Written Project Plan

Each project should have specific and measurable objectives that will be accomplished in at least four areas. First, the project objectives should specify the performance improvement to be achieved in the business process. Improvement should be expressed as either increased profits or realized reduced costs. Second, the project should be broken down into tasks. Third, the objectives should specify the resources that will be required for each task in the project. These resources will include people (including skills), technology (hardware and software), and dollars. Fourth, the objectives should provide a definite time line for completion of the various tasks involved in the project. The objectives, tasks, resources, and completion time are included as the key components of the project plan.

This project plan should be written down, distributed, and agreed to by the project team. It is critical that every member of the project team has access to these measurable objectives and agrees that they are achievable. As the project progresses, interim measures should be specified and displayed so that all can follow the progress being made toward successful completion of the project.

Step 4: Prototype

Most information systems managers, when developing a computer-based information system, strive to get it right the first time. But, given the complexities of the project (the interaction that must go on between people, databases, communications interfaces, and other information systems), perfection is rarely possible.

I've found that I'm usually faced with two options: Either I can get the team to work to perfection the first time, or I can plan for imperfection and work to get to the desired state in several improvement iterations.

Here's an example of the iteration process. I want my information system to achieve at least 99 percent accuracy. My information systems managers tell me that they can easily achieve 80 percent accuracy on the first try and eliminate 80 percent of any remaining error rate on any subsequent iteration. Under this process, I can accomplish my 99 percent accuracy objective with three iterations. Assume that iteration one achieves 80 percent accuracy. Iteration two removes 80 percent of the 20 percent initial errors, or 16 percent, to arrive at 96 percent accuracy. Finally, iteration three removes 80 percent of the remaining 4 percent error rate. I now have accomplished my target of a system with 99.2 percent accuracy/uptime.

An 80 percent error rate would be totally unacceptable for a finished system, but 80 percent is great for a prototype. If I'm going to achieve my 90- to 120-day completion target, using a prototype with several iterations to achieve an acceptable finished system becomes the preferred alternative. Because technology is changing so quickly in today's world, perfection in the initial product is rarely achievable. In this environment, using a prototype with several improvement iterations is now an acceptable alternative. Besides, it's a lot easier to make a quick first pass and then work with the whole team to create the acceptable 99 percent accuracy.

Perhaps because I'm a manager interested in moving quickly, using a prototype has always made sense to me. However, I've often encountered high resistance to using a prototype. Most of my technologists usually want perfection. But, given the rate of change in the world today, I see perfection as just a momentary illusion at best. I can't avoid change in my information systems. I need to embrace and support change in the technologies that support my organization. Just ten years ago, talking about change this way would have been extremely scary.

Step 5: Implementation Is Completion

Step 5 is the easiest step to implement. It occurs naturally. After prototyping the system, involve everyone and receive their input. After several iterations, we should see the desired results. The project objectives that specify the improvement in the business process have been accomplished. The technology and business objectives and profit or cost-reduction objectives have been achieved to the extent possible for this project. The accomplishment is at least at a level acceptable to the business process manager, the IT professional, and the whole project team. At this point, the system is celebrated as finished. The implementation is completed. Enjoy this moment!

Step 6: Continual Process Improvement

I must not think of my evolving information systems as given, completed, and unchanging. As a manager, I need to focus on the continual improvement process in my information systems. Evaluate your technical and business process accomplishments in detail at this time. How did you do?

This is not nirvana. This is not the end. Just as I now recognize that a continual improvement process is necessary to keep current the product or service I provide to my customers, I must also recognize continual process improvement in information systems.

With the completion of Step 5, you may think that you're able to leave technology implementation alone for the next five, ten, or twenty years. No way! By making this assumption, many large organizations have reached a crisis point with their information systems. These mega-organizations find their computerized information systems limping along, needing changes that appear overwhelmingly difficult. But they need business process improvement to maintain customer satisfaction or competitive cost structure. Their old legacy systems are no longer effective, but the task of changing them appears almost insurmountable.

Continuous change and improvement must be the order of the day. Rapidly changing PC technology is affecting all areas of computing and communications technology. Technology is now becoming obsolete in a period of six to eighteen months.

New Technology Creates New Opportunities

To take advantage of this improving technology, we'll always be involved in the continuous improvement process. I'm not saying that everything must change. Rather, we need to be in a continuous process of evaluating what we have accomplished while also evaluating areas in which improving technology has potential to enhance our business processes. Continuous improvement becomes a state of mind in the organization, whereby we're always looking at the critical areas of our business process to find opportunities for improvement.

Step 3, setting a limited scope for the project, and Step 4, using a prototype, are both directed at creating a process of continual change and improvement. Continual improvement has now entered the world of information systems that have become critical to our organizations.

Step 7: Communication, Communication, Communication

We now circle back to Step 1, cultural change focusing on clear and honest communication in the implementation team. No matter how much emphasis is put on communications, it usually turns out to be a problem.

Remember—don't shoot the messenger. An information systems manager simply doesn't like to tell the business manager that the project he or she has been working on is a failure, that the project didn't meet all the anticipated business process, financial, and technical objectives.

Here's the situation: What looked promising several months ago is going nowhere. The project needs to be scrapped in favor of a new approach. Here's the problem: The boss-subordinate problem of the organizational hierarchy discussed in Step 1 is compounded by the nature of the relationship between the IS manager and the business manager.

News of a failure or a dead end is the most critical information that I need as a manager. At the same time, such information is the most difficult to gather in a timely fashion. In my experience, the only way I have found to engender willingness in my subordinates to tell me the truth when it is bad news is to discuss this possibility openly as we start a project. To encourage openness, I've stressed these points: The implementation of new technology is by definition risky; failures are to be expected; the possibility of not achieving acceptable project objectives must be recognized. If project failure occurs, it must be confirmed and acknowledged by everyone on the team. I will address this in more detail in Chapter 13.

Implementing Technology Is a Continual Improvement Process

Technology change and its impact on our organizations keep accelerating.

A continual improvement process must be in place. Here again is the model:

1. Create a project culture.

2. Describe and display the desired business process.

3. Develop the technical scope, including both a technical and financial evaluation.

4. Introduce the prototype.

5. Modify the system to achieve acceptable technical and business objectives.

6. Evaluate a continuous improvement process.

7. Remember—communicate, communicate, communicate!

After going through all the seven steps, go back to Step 1. The process goes through all the steps again. Improvement is the never-ending quest. Perfection does not exist. You can always make additional changes that create value to the "customer" and result in an improved business process.

CHAPTER 8

MIS Process Methodology: "Intrapreneuring"

by Bill Bysinger

" LAN'S are definitely the way to go. All my friends are installing them in their companies."

"This new technology is great! It runs four times as fast as our current hardware."

"We have a list of projects that will keep us busy for at least four years."

"We can do anything you want for that new sale support system. Just tell me."

Are you saying you can do anything???!!!

I know that I am part of the problem. I often do not challenge the technologist to make sure that what they are doing makes economic sense for the organization. When I hear their outlandish statements or promises I often just roll my eyes and say nothing. Not good!

In this chapter, Bill conveys the zeal and enthusiasm that I should look for as I get my technologists to move through the seven-step process that leads to continual business-process change. He emphasizes the passion of the technologist to address the business problem so that a return in the form of increased profits or reduced costs can be created.

> *What a pleasure it is when my technological professionals focus on the business process, participate in the scope definition that generates financial as well as technical returns, take the steps to get it done, quickly adjust to the required modifications as the information systems are implemented, and then see that they are part of a continual process of creating improvements. Clear communication with all of us in the organization is essential throughout. This is it, the continual improvement process.*
>
> *Ken Knight*

Ken just finished talking about how to manage information systems projects for continual improvement. In this chapter, I'll detail the methodology further and give tangible examples of successful projects in "intrapreneurial" terms. "Intrapreneuring" is attracting company funding to deliver technology that enables the company's business process.

For technology to have an effective impact on the business, a methodology for enabling technology into the business must be built and deployed. This methodology cannot be bought; it must be developed as a cultural imperative in the business.

The key to making a methodology successful is "evangelism." What is "evangelism?" It is the impassioned selling of ideas and concepts. The ability to sell your ideas is not based only on generating information. Selling requires skillful presentation. Presentation must be visually pleasing but, even more so, the visually pleasing information must be delivered with passion.

IN SALES, PASSION IS THE KEY TO SUCCESS

In my experience as an IS manager, a field in which passion is rarely mentioned, I've found that the ability to make speeches that thrill audiences pays off consistently. I've learned that the art of oratory is not limited to the Abraham Lincolns, Clarence Darrows, and John F. Kennedys of this world; it's the most important tool that technology managers in the 1990s can draw from their tool kits.

I have no fear of overselling the usefulness of this powerful talent. I use this sales tool every day in my responsibility for guiding the use of technology in my company. I find that, if you believe in what you do, you'll become passionate about it. Your passion will get others excited about it.

Some years ago, I was chartered to help bring more PCs into the mainstream business processing of my company. This may seem strange for an IS director, but we had a unique environment. We had about 650 employees worldwide and more than 1500 personal computers. Most of these personal workstations were Macintosh. Everyone had a Mac on her/his desk, even if she/he also had a DOS or OS2 PC. Our networks and office automation products for word processing, spreadsheet, and mail had been built on an existing Mac environment. The Mac environment caused considerable problems for those who had a passion for DOS and OS2. The primary problems we experienced were sending attached enclosures over the network from Macs to PCs and remote printing in color.

A Major Opportunity

I saw this project as a major opportunity. I could help the PC-user minority by championing their cause while simultaneously moving the company to our PCs. However, I didn't know that these users had heard this call to action twice before. The only results were talk, but no action. Every time I sent a message from my Mac, I got nothing but caustic remarks back from many PC users. (One of the dangers of electronic mail is quick response—the send key is sometimes quicker than the brain.) After too many mail responses back and forth, I contacted a manager of the largest disgruntled group. When I asked her for a meeting, she agreed. She sounded ready to bury the hatchet—in me.

The day of the meeting arrived. I was prepared to get killed, but I thought, "Maybe if I tell this group why I think PCs should be strategic workstations for the company, they'll think before they fire." I explained my impassioned opinion about the significance of PCs for the business. I told them that I, like they, wanted to use a PC as easily as I had been using my Mac. I said that I was prepared to help build the architecture to make it happen.

Their response? The senior member of the group said, "You've disarmed us by telling us that you care as much as we do about PCs becoming important to the company." The result of this meeting? I gained many allies who wanted to help make this project successful.

The ability to influence groups through good presentation and speaking skills cannot be oversold. If you haven't given any thought to your presentation skills and feel you lack these abilities, take a Dale Carnegie course or a class on effective presentations and public speaking. Over the years, I have found these skills to be the key ingredient to my success. I love making presentations and passing my enthusiasm for the implementation of technology on to others. Nothing is more energizing than to have a group get excited about your ideas and experiences.

Now that we've discussed the need for evangelism and passion in your communication with business users, let's develop the rest of the story on methodology. *Methodology* is a $1,000 word for process. The problem here is that most IS people think of methodology as a way to write code. This, however, is not true. Methodology is a way to uncover real need in the business.

Methodology is a process based on the reengineering efforts and changes in the way we do business in a company. I emphasize however, that this is a journey, not a destination. Methodology has to be iterated; it must be dynamic; and it must be internalized in the daily business process.

CREATE A VISION OF WHAT YOUR ORGANIZATION WILL LOOK LIKE

Methodology begins with a vision of what you believe your world will look like in three to five years. A simple list of future technology or business needs will suffice:

- Distribute videos and images in an electronic product catalog
- Provide telecommuting opportunities for the company's workforce
- Improve process and provide for greater information dissemination
- Build a global presence for the business

If you have responsibility for technology in your company, what does vision mean for you? It means that everything you do and all the technology you deploy had better be moving to make these visions happen. You can do this by understanding your business process and your customers' needs. You need to go to the market—(your internal customers)—to find out how these visions can help them solve their problems.

A number of years ago, I was recruited by a fast-growing company to be their first real IS director. During my first ninety days with this company, I wandered around talking to as many people as would respond. Many didn't have time to talk; some thought I was wasting their time; and others saw me as an opportunity to tell their hard luck stories. After all the digging, however, I uncovered major opportunities for IS to show real value to the business.

My IS organization capitalized on these opportunities. We created a published process that showed how we were going to understand the business better and how we were going to help our customers determine when technology could help them. Then we took some process modeling information from a quality class that everyone in the company had to attend, some product management principles from another corporate-sponsored class, some cost-benefit training that I had learned as a finance manager and in my industrial engineering training, and some clarity training from another corporate-sponsored class, and put them together to build our first methodology. This became a model for how we were going to talk to our customers, scope projects, manage projects, and deploy technologies.

After this exercise, we were able to create some models that helped our customers help us to be successful (and that shocked the company). These models were as follow:

- All technology projects were targeted to be completed in ninety days (eighteen weeks). Since our corporate measurements were based on quarterly results, this made sense to us.

- All technology projects had to be based on business need.

- All technology projects had to show measurable return in less than one year, and payoffs of two to three times the cost in twelve months following implementation and start-up.

In my first year of using this model, I presented it to a local chapter of the Society for Information Management (SIM), and many of the members told me I was on a suicide mission. Surprisingly enough, three years later almost to the day, I made an updated presentation to SIM on how successful this effort had been. Many members wanted to know how to do it.

There is nothing magic about this process. If a project's requirements are well understood and the project is scoped to a finite time frame, results are readily achievable. The main difficulties are that most IS people don't know how to scope and they can't prevent feature creep.

HOW TO BE SUCCESSFUL

I will give you three initial hints for how to be successful. Then you need to spend more time looking into this process than we have here.

1. Set a stake on time frames. I suggest picking half the time frame you're currently using. For example, if you have eighteen-month projects, change the time frame to nine months.

2. Ask the users to rank-order by priority the features and functions they need. They should also assign cost-benefit values to those functions to show which give the greatest bang for the buck. You could ask users, if they could pick only twenty-five features or functions, which would they be?

3. Always make sure that you have a senior executive sponsor committed to the project's risk and success. Such commitment will solve the resource problem and also make sure that the project is viable. Too many projects are requested that have no real impact on the business.

    There are many more issues, but these are the top three.

RETURNS FROM INFORMATION TECHNOLOGY INVESTMENTS— INCREASE PROFITS OR REDUCED COSTS

A methodology allows for successful "intrapreneuring." Remember, IS has no money. Your customers have the money. If they can lend you some, you can double or triple their investments by delivering technology that enables better process, provides increased business opportunities, or allows for more output without increasing staff resources. Here are some examples of payback:

- Sales systems should be paid for through a percentage of every sale that has resulted from improvements in market penetration or closing process through the use of a sales system.

- Manufacturing system improvement through technology should equate to lowering manufacturing costs or increasing output.

- Service systems are paid for by increased service contracts or efficiencies in the cost of servicing a customer.

Financial information systems are also a good illustration of payback. If you are a publicly held company, reporting your results early can increase your earnings per share. This is another benefit from technology measured in hard dollars.

No system should be justified by reducing head count. Rather, the system should be justified because it doesn't increase head count as quickly as other options or because it shows real dollar increases in business. The key to a good methodology is measurability. The measures used should set a clear horizon that isn't affected by major business change that would mask the value of the investment.

Evangelism, passion, process, scope, "intrapreneuring," and value—these are what make methodology important. Process understanding is power in business because process is business. The better it is, the better it does. Process isn't something in a three-ring binder; it's a living process that changes as you learn how to get better at it through iteration.

Who better to empower process than the keepers of the technology tools?

INFORMATION SYSTEMS BUSINESS PROCESS METHODOLOGY

Phases	Process	Processes and Responsibilities	
		Single-point accountable	Team or persons involved
1	Information systems technology framework (technology vision for the company)	Information systems executive	Information systems organization
2	Technology vision sold to company executive	Information systems executives	Information systems management
3	Create and publish project parameters	Information systems executive	Information systems management

Phases	Processes and Responsibilities (cont.)		
	Process	Single-point accountable	Team or persons involved
4	Identify opportunities in a business unit	Information systems management	Business managers
5	Simple project proposal	Business management	Users
6	Project estimate/ benefits analysis	Business management/ information systems management	Users
7	Business sponsor created	Business executive and IS executive	CEO and/or COO
8	Business benefit articulated in tangible measurements	Business and IS executives	CEO, COO, CFO
9	Project team created	Business management/ information systems management	Business unit and information systems
10	Project manager appointed	Management assignees, may be from business or IS	Business unit
11	Formal project brief created and published	Project manager	Project team
12	Project brief sign-off	Project manager	Information systems and business executive
13	Project success measurement established	Project manager	Project team
14	Project approval and commencement	Project manager	Business and IS executives

CHAPTER 9

Technical Value: Measuring Return on Investment

by Ken Knight

"The most difficult part of my job is always getting funding for projects and resources. The CEO and CFO never understand that I serve the company and I need the resources to be successful."

"The company gets bigger, takes on more products, buys subsidiaries, and the last thing they consider is the MIS costs. They want everything quick and at no cost. I remember when we opened that new distribution plant we acquired, the MIS cost was not scientifically calculated, it was based on some arbitrary percentage from the accounting department."

"If only the business managers would get me involved earlier and let me participate in the business decisions on cost of expansion."

"Most MIS executives must perform miracles in fast growing companies. It is always an early Monday morning when they get the word that a major acquisition has been made or a major expansion decision has been targeted. Without being asked for input, MIS is given a delivery date and a directive to "Make It Happen."

118   Investing in Information Technology

> *In this chapter Ken resets the thinking regarding technology investment as a business model and how ROI on technology should be viewed. This is a pragmatic view at how a businessman should understand the real value from investments in technology and not as a cost that is necessary in the running of the company. Technology investments need to be leveraged.*
>
> *Bill Bysinger*

In Chapter 7, we saw that the third step in the process for creating continuous improvement consists of developing a technical scope that produces value for the organization. Today, most organizations are investing heavily in technology, computer, communications, and other information systems. What are we getting from those investments?

From my years of experience, it has become clear that I must manage the organization's technology to make sure that it, along with other investments, creates an adequate return on that investment. Unfortunately, return on investment has all too often been neglected by us as organizational executives.

ORGANIZATIONS TEND TO TREAT TECHNOLOGY AS A UTILITY

During the past twenty-five years, I've been involved with many large organizations. From my observations of the computer operations in these firms, I conclude that they tend to act the way those in electric utilities do. That is, the information systems group fights for its annual budget. Its budget request may be based on what it feels "technically" has to be accomplished in the organization next year. More likely, the budget is based on a formula—an annual percentage increase or a percentage of the total organization's revenues.

Once the computer budget is established, the various operational groups make their requests for system improvements. Soon, a long list of requests far outstrips the computer department's ability to complete them in the budget year. The computer department next decides which projects will be done when. Then they work to deliver the projects.

The utility-type computer groups achieved consistent results—consistently poor, I'm sad to say. They delivered information systems far later than originally promised. The delivered systems didn't meet the requirements of the business process managers. Their "finished products" were way over budget. Such consistent outcomes were a major source of frustration to me as a manager.

The computer group's greatest success was building a wall around itself. Its borders were marked by signs reading, "This is my turf. Stay away." I now recognize that I created this problem. I allowed the group to set up its own kingdom. Then the group separated itself emotionally from the rest of the organization. Behind their wall, the members of the group developed a mind-set that they knew best because they were the computer experts.

Now that I think about it, my response was interesting. I didn't want to go behind that wall because I wasn't comfortable there. My hindsight tells me that I was fostering the view that my computer operations were a "computer utility." I didn't demand the same management control and accountability of the computer group that I expected of my other functional groups. I created the problem and I needed to solve it.

Today, I often observe computer groups operating within their companies as if they are independent utilities. Corporate management becomes frustrated. Rather than take charge, they fire the information systems manager and hire a new one. Management feel that this is their only course of action. As a result, the position of information officer is currently experiencing rapid turnover in medium and large organizations. Unfortunately, firing the person in charge of computer operations doesn't solve the underlying management problem. The vicious circle of unimproved business process, blown budgets, and late deliveries continues with the new IS manager.

We are entering an era in which corporations use technology to create distinctiveness and competitive advantage. Ironically, at the same time, managers are concerned that their computer experts are ineffective. Is a high level of technological incompetence the source of the problem? No. The technology training available today has never been better. The individuals entering the computer and communications field are among our best and brightest. The problem lies with us as managers: We created the problem and we're the ones who are going to have to solve it.

THINK OF TECHNOLOGY AS AN INVESTMENT

We need to stop fooling ourselves. Investment in technology is just like any other investment in our organizations. As managers of the business process, we need to oversee and coordinate process, just as we do the other major human and financial commitments of our firms.

During my tenure as a business school dean, I've seen business schools create departments of finance, marketing, sales, accounting, human resources, insurance, operations, real estate, international business, operations research, and business strategy. Schools have brought computers into our instruction and may even introduce an exam that assures that graduating students are computer-literate. But schools still lack an approach to the management of computers and communications as a technological management process. Only a few universities have added information systems management courses to their curricula, and only within the past five years. I have seen a similar slowness to realize the importance of information systems management in businesses. It doesn't come as much of a surprise that most of today's business graduates want to avoid managing information systems within their organizations.

Leave Budget Responsibility to Business Process Managers

The firm's first step toward setting appropriate management responsibilities for information systems is to eliminate the computer department as a stand-alone "utility." Take the budget from the computer group and return it to the individual business process managers. Tell the computer professionals that they are going to join development teams. The project teams will develop the project scope, including desired improvements to the business process, tasks to be performed, project cost, and completion schedule. Put the business manager in clear control of the IS budget, such that the business manager authorizes IS expenditures. The business manager holds the technologist accountable for project progress and outcome.

Thus, the information systems budget would no longer be left to the discretion of the technologist. Since the budget is now controlled by the business managers, the business process manager decides what to spend on maintenance and investment in improvement. For his or her part, the technologist specifies performance and the improvement that can be achieved. The two work together as key directors of the project team to assure that money spent on technology makes a difference to the organization. Their main job is making sure that every dollar spent enhances the business process. Together, they see to it that the technology implemented makes the desired contributions to the organization.

As budget control shifts to the business manager, the budget should also shift, with its weight moving away from maintenance. The majority of the company's dollars and effort should be devoted instead to the development of systems improvements.

Technology Is Like Any Other Investment

Managers must view their investments in information technology just as they view any other investment. If managers are going to be responsible for the business process, they need to know what each investment is going to cost and what return to expect. This represents a clear shift away from the computer group acting like a utility.

The manager who let the computer group follow the utility model paid the group fees and utilized whatever was provided. The manager gave the group a wish list and then let the "utility" do its thing. The manager acted under the assumption that the computer group knew what was best and that the group, made up as it was of technologists, would do what was right.

The problem was lack of communication. The manager didn't provide the computer group with the insight and information it needed to assess how the new information technology would benefit the business process.

To illustrate this problem, let me recount an incident that occurred when I was CEO of Wm. B. Wilson. I asked my technologists to rearrange my monthly financial statements to facilitate a quick estimate of each division's gross contribution. I thought my request was very reasonable since it took me an extra couple of minutes each month to calculate each division's percentage. I needed to look closely at these percentages—they gave me an early warning if direct costs were changing.

My computer group responded like a utility. It took me at my word and set out to make the program changes I requested. It didn't ask how much the change was worth to me. Nor did it tell me the cost in time and effort to complete the modification.

After two months, the computer group brought me the revised financial report. It was exactly what I had requested. I almost cheered—they'd gotten it right this time! After I thanked the technologist, I made a big mistake: I asked how many hours of work were involved in the improvement. The technologist answered with a smile, "About 150 hours of programmer time."

Wow! Had I made a bad investment! I spent 150 programmer hours to save two minutes per month. This investment would never pay back.

I wish that I could say that our low-return investments were limited to small (150-hour) spending sprees. But I remember a several-man-year rewrite of the customer database at Creative Publications, Inc., that produced no business process improvement whatsoever. It did make the output look better, but at excessive cost.

After several such incidents, an insight finally penetrated my thick skull: I needed to view changes to information systems as I viewed any other investment by Wm. B. Wilson. My responsibility was to communicate the potential benefit the change would bring. It was also up to me to ask how much the modification would cost.

I need to look at all the costs the proposed improvement involves. Costs include the PCs on my employees' desks and the software inside the PCs. When my technologists begin distributing computing and server environments, I need to be even more careful about costs. Many parts of the total cost of my information system can become hidden as they are buried in the budgets of the firm's functional divisions.

Demand a Return on Investments in Technology

After seeing how easy it is to make poor technology investments, I now approach each potential investment demanding an acceptable return. The manager's first step is to initiate a procedure for examining anticipated benefits carefully. The manager asks the question: Which benefits will accrue from implementation of the new technology? Most of the information that answers this question will be supplied by the business process managers. The manager must make clear to the business process managers that the benefits cited in their responses should be specific and quantifiable.

To begin considering these benefits, the manager has to count the cost. The manager's next question is: How much investment in terms of the company's human and financial resources is required for this technological change? Because the technologists are in the best position to understand the complexity of the project and, hence, the expenditures involved, the manager gives them the first crack at a cost estimate. The business managers add in costs to their operations. Business process costs should include the personnel time used to develop the project. Disruption of the business process during the prototyping and other implementation steps of the project should also be included as part of total costs. If either the benefits or the costs cannot be defined to the mutual satisfaction of both the business managers and the technologists, do not proceed. Go back to redefine the project's scope until the benefits and costs can be defined and mutually agreed on. Proceed further only when it appears that an acceptable return on the technology investment will be realized. I'll discuss acceptable return in more detail later in this chapter. Obviously, desired return won't always be achieved. My point here is that if you don't see a clear belief that the return is possible, don't start the project.

Expect a Quick Payback on Technology Investments

How critical is the time factor in calculating return on technology investments? *Very critical!*

I'm usually tempted to calculate the return on an information system technology over a useful life of five or more years. I tend to think that if the new technology creates an improvement with financial benefits today, the benefits will continue over the life of the computer equipment.

But this thinking doesn't apply in the present environment. Computer and communication technology is improving so rapidly that it is now impossible to forecast potential benefits from technology to my business process, even one or two years from now. I've learned from experience in this environment that it is better to keep timelines short. Anyone introducing new technology needs to realize returns almost immediately. Performance per dollar paid for computer and communication technology is increasing 50 percent to 100 percent annually. Such performance isn't limited to hardware. Although the data isn't as widely published, software performance is also improving at exponential rates. Two sources of programming productivity improvements are the use of object-oriented programming and the reuse of program segments in object libraries. New programming languages such as Visual Basic and Visual

C++ are another source of programming productivity improvement.

Given the uncertainty generated by such rapid technology improvement, I question the sophisticated rate-of-return calculations that my associates at leading U.S. business schools have been teaching. The uncertainty created by this rapid performance improvement in information systems technology makes traditional rate-of-return calculations relatively useless.

I think I've found a more useful alternative. I look at payback for a good indicator of investment return. Payback is the length of time it takes to recover the investment. In a world in which technology improvements are exploding, I'm suspicious of payback periods longer than six to twelve months.

Technology Investment Modeling

The following are models to be used in making decisions on acquiring or building technology. The message is simple: investments must always produce an adequate financial return on investment (ROI) in technology and process:

ROI = three times the cost savings over twelve to twenty-four months
  = twofold time increase in profits over twelve to twenty-four months

The key is to use the investment model as a tracking device to justify the investment over time and ensure the return achieved. Let's look at an example. We will go over another illustration utilizing the same model at the end of Chapter 8.

What Are the Elements of a Cost-Savings Model?

First, describe the benefits to the business:

Example: An insurance company can replace a technology that consists of twenty steps to process a customer's new insurance policy with one that has only four steps. In doing so, the company will be able to create a better way to process new insurance policies by cutting down the response time to the customer from fifteen days to two days. The insurance company will also save money and reduce costs in the revised and simplified business process.

Second, quantify the cost savings:

Measurements	Current Process	New Process
Average cost per hour (New process requires higher-wage-rate staff.)	$25.00	$30.00

Staff hours based on 50 weeks

Finance	200 hr	
Underwriting	500	
Customer service	2,350	
Sales	650	
Credit	1,221	
Total	4,921 hrs	

The new process, with twenty steps reduced by sixteen, is able to reduce the person-hours by 70 percent, for a result of 1,476 hours saved.

Annual operating costs	<u>$123,025</u>	<u>$44,280</u>
Associated costs:		
Telephone	$10,100 (reduce by 50%)	$ 5,050
Forms	19,250 (reduce by 60%)	9,625
Travel	35,000 (reduce by 50%)	17,500
Subtotal	<u>$187,375</u>	<u>$76,455</u>
MIS costs increased in support	_____	<u>14,600</u>
Total Costs	$187,375	$91,055

Annual savings if new information system in place this year: $96,320

Total insurance policies processed (current): 9,540

	Current Process	New Process
Cost of processing a return	$19.64	$9.55

Projected returns for next year 10,494

Cost of processing projected returns	$206,102	$100,218

Projected savings next year $105,884

This saving (given the saving investment model) would substantiate the following technology investment:

3:1 return in 12 months	$32,107 investment
3:1 return in 18 months	$49,754 investment
3.1 return in 24 months	$67,401 investment

Each of these investments should be closely tracked to substantiate the expected return.

Alternately, let's look at a revenue/earnings increase model.

First, describe the benefits to the business:

Too often we confuse revenue with earnings. Concentrate on earnings!

Example: Getting product to market is time-critical. Often, the difference between market leader and poor second is the rate at which a firm can introduce its product. If we could provide technology to create information to get the products to market quicker or to generate a process that will help get a product to market quicker, even by a few months, this might produce an exceptional return on the information systems technology enabler. Not only does the product have early sales, but it starts the growth curve and thus generates additional sales each month.

Second, quantify the additional profits to be earned:

Measurement	Current Process	New Process
Product time to market	12 months	8 months
Product price:	$395.00	

Projected sales (assuming that the product would be introduced at the end of the first year under the current process and that the new process will produce a four-month lead):

	0 months	4 months
Units sold first year:	0	7,000
Future sales:		
Second year	28,000	36,000
Third year	40,000	49,000

Incremental increase in sales:

First year 7,000 units
Next six months 15,000 units

Total increase in sales for 16 months: 22,000 units

Revenue generated in the first twelve months of the originally planned product introduction as a result of increasing the delivery to market by four months:

$$22,000 \times \$395 = \$8,690,000$$

If the product margin on the product is 25 percent, this would be the additional profit earned in the first year of originally planned sales as a result of increasing the delivery to market by four months.

Additional anticipated twelve-month earnings: $2,172,500

First-year earnings using the new technology to accelerate the introduction by four months would justify an investment of $1,086,250 to achieve the targeted 2:1 return in twelve months.

In presenting our Technology Investment Models we have included one example of a Cost-Savings Model and one of a Profit Increase Model. The concepts in these models are not dependent upon the size of the organization or the amount of the investment. I continually run across situations that demonstrate the value of thinking in this framework for both large corporate technology investments and the investments being made by the single user. To further illustrate this, let's explore two additional examples for each of the two Technology Investment Models.

Two Examples of a Cost-Savings Model

The simple message: technology investments must always produce an adequate financial return on investment (ROI) in technology and process: ROI = three times the cost savings over twelve to twenty-four months. The Cost-Savings Model becomes a tracking device. First it justifies the investment and the it substantiates that the anticipated return has been achieved.

Let's look at two new examples of the Cost-Savings Model.

Example One—A large aerospace manufacturing firm invests in a new integrated manufacturing system.

First element of the model—describe the benefits to the business:

A large aerospace firm wrestles with the problem of having over five hundred legacy systems that must share data to provide the computing support necessary to produce its products. Many of these systems date back more than 30 years. The systems are written in many different computer languages and written to run on computer systems that have long been discarded. The systems are extremely cumbersome.

One aspect of the problem is that the computer systems contain different part numbering systems. The data structures and formats are not compatible with many to one (or one to many) conversations. Therefore, there is a lack of electronic connectibility. These legacy systems cannot communicate with each other.

The result is that several thousand staff members from the computer support and engineering support groups must devote 100 percent of their time to get the legacy systems to work together. Like so many large organizations today, total conversion to a single integrated seamless design to manufacture systems seems appropriate. The benefits will be a greatly improved manufacturing process, a reduction in the required rework, and a reduction in computer and engineering support staff.

Second element of the model–quantify the cost savings:

Measurements	Current Process	New Process
Average cost per hour (New process requires higher-wage-rate staff.)	$45.00	$55.00

Staff hours based on 50 weeks

Computer support	4,575,000 hr	
Engineering support	21,790,000 hr	
Total	7,365,000 hrs	

The new process with a movement from 500+ legacy systems to a single integrated system will reduce the support requirements by 85 percent or an estimated 6,260,250 hours.

Annual labor costs:	$331,425,000	$60,765,250

Associated costs: space, travel, equipment and supplies, communications

reduced by 70%	$45,950,000	$13,785,000
Total Costs	$377,375,000	$74,550,250

Annual savings if new information system in place this year:	$302,824,750
Investment to purchase/build and implement the new system:	$197,875,000
Projected returns for second year	**$353,824,750**

This savings (given the Cost-Savings Model) would be as follows:

3:1 return in 12 months $100,941,583 investment
3:1 return in 18 months $159,912,375 investment
3:1 return in 24 months $218,883,166 investment

This return would substantiate the technology investment on the basis of an acceptable return within a projected 24 month period. Each investment should be closely tracked to substantiate that the expected return has been achieved.

Example Two—A one person computer laptop repair business invests in QuickBooks system.

First element of the model—describes the benefits to the business:

A close friend, Dave Lindstrom, acquired a business to repair a private labeled version of a 386 laptop computer. These laptops were sold to large corporations in substantial numbers. Dave had a staff of only two people to perform his repair service. He purchased all components and contracted out the electronic repair and assembly work.

The problem that Dave faced was how to keep good records of all aspects of the business to best manage this part-time business and provide the most valued service to his customers. Starting with paper and card files Dave found that it took him an average of one hour to do all the paperwork associated with the service order and corporate records. The paperwork included providing a written estimate prior to repairs, creating bill and shipping materials, keeping track of accounts receivable including recording receipts, entering the transaction information into his general ledger and preparing monthly financial statements.

This one hour per service still did not give him the easy ability to answer other questions such as what other laptops from this same firm have I serviced, and when. What type of repairs, and how many, have I done in the last two months and how does that compare with an earlier historical period.

Dave felt that the could give himself better information with which to manage his business as well as saving himself time if the went from a manual system to QuickBooks.

Second element of the model—quantify the cost savings:

Measurements	Current Process	New Process
Average cost per hour (Dave set this as the value of his time.)	$40/hr	$40/hr
Dave's hours based on 12 repairs per week	$480/wk	
Total Current Annual Costs	$24,960	

Dave projected that QuickBooks would reduce the average amount of paperwork that he would do to 20 minutes per repair service.

Dave's revised paperwork hours on 12 repairs per week with QuickBooks:
    $26.67 per repair for a total of $160/wk

Total Annualized Costs with QuickBooks $8,320

Annual savings if new information system, QuickBooks, is used: $16,640

Investment to purchase/build and implement QuickBooks:
    Purchase new computer and printer $3,695
    Purchase QuickBooks   150
    Dave's setup/training time (27 hours)   <u>1,080</u>
    Total investment $4,925

For the second year Dave anticipates that the rate of repairs would decrease to 9 per week. This yields a projected savings in year two of $12,480.

This savings (given the Cost-Savings Model) would be as follows:

    3:1 return in 12 months $5,547 investment
    3:1 return in 18 months $11,787 investment
    3:1 return in 24 months $18,027 investment

This return would substantiate the technology investment on the basis of an acceptable return with a projected 12 month period. Dave should follow his actual savings to substantiate that the expected savings of 40 minutes per repair service has been achieved.

Two Examples of the Profit Increase Model

Again my message is simple: technology investments must always produce an adequate financial return on investment (ROI) in technology and process: ROI = two times the increase in profits over twelve to twenty-four months. The Profit Increase Model becomes a tracking device. First it justifies the technology investment and then substantiates that the anticipated return has been achieved.

Let's look at two new examples of the profit Increase Model.

Example One—A large northwest automobile dealership invests in a world wide web (WWW) Homepage.

First element of the model—describe the benefits to the business:

Remember that too often we confuse revenue with earnings. Concentrate on profits!

A Northwest automobile dealership was one of the early organizations that saw the potential to increase business through the world wide web. The dealership established a domain address and set up a series of pages on its homepage that provided information on its new and used cars as well as information on purchasing parts of the vehicle brands it sold. The owner/manager felt that the emerging world wide web offered him a unique opportunity to attract new and different new and used car customers and to provide parts on an overnight basis to customers anywhere in the U.S. The owner felt that this would represent new business at the same gross margins as now being achieved. This would provide additional revenue for overhead and profit.

Second, quantify the additional profits to be earned:

The implementation of the new Homepage was anticipated to produce a modest increase in business during the first year that it was put in place.

	GROSS PROFIT IN DOLLARS
Measurement	Use of WWW
Additional new and used car sales (+1)	$500
Additional parts sales	$2,000
Additional gross profits first year:	$30,000
Future additional gross profit:	
Second year	$45,000
Third year	$60,000
Cost to establish, maintain and update the Homepage.	
Additional computer equipment	$ 750
Develop and implement the Homepage	$9,100
Total technology investment	$9,850
Cost to maintain the Homepage $650/month with an annual commitment on the maintenance contract.	$7,800
Total cost during the first year	$17,650
Total cost during the first 18 months	$21,550
Total cost during the first 24 months	$21,400

This results in the following increase in gross profits;

Year one	$12,350
First 18 months	$30,950
Year one and two	$49,500

This increase in profits (given the Profits Increase Model) would support a technology investment as follows:

2:1 return in 12 months	$6,175 investment
2:1 return in 18 months	$15,475 investment
2:1 return in 24 months	$24,750 investment

Gross profits using the new world wide web Homepage technology to increase automobile and parts sales would justify the $9,950 investment and additional monthly costs to achieve the targeted 2:1 return within eighteen months.

By utilizing this model, we have explored the value of the technology to see if we do expect to increase earnings. As technologists, we all too often overlook this aspect of technology acquisition.

As an interesting aside in this situation, the new distribution channel on the world wide web itself became very valuable and had a significant value in addition to the increased profits to the automobile dealership.

Example Two—An independent mortgage broker develops a newsletter to increase her customer network.

First element of the model—describe the benefits to the business:

June went back into the mortgage brokerage business about 12 months ago. After a slow start-up period it became apparent to her that it was necessary for her to get her message out to her many friends—"they should think of June first for their mortgage needs" and then contact her as they needed to obtain mortgage financing their home or investment property. While June was well known in the Seattle community she had not been in mortgage brokerage for over ten years. This required a powerful and cost effective way to get her business network to contact her for their mortgage needs. June had the information technology to produce a newsletter. She already had a good 486 computer system, laser printer, and Microsoft Word with its newsletter template. The only technology left that June had to invest in was establishing her newsletter format and style and learning how to generate the monthly newsletter.

Through this newsletter June felt that she could be very effective in presenting her image as the mortgage broker that is on top of this dynamically changing market, knowledgeable about the requirements of the lenders she represented, and the "can-do" individual who would get the job done.

Second, quantify the additional profits to be earned:

June felt the implementation of the newsletter would double the amount of her business during the first two years that it was published.

Measurement	Current Process	Newsletter
Total mortgage revenues:		
1996	$25,000	$50,000
1997	$45,000	$90,000

Since June had adequate free time she placed a low value (cost) on her time. She felt that her time was worth no more than $10/hour and that the development of the newsletter and mailing list would be 250 hours.

	0	$2,500

The cost of publishing and distributing 1,000 monthly newsletters for twelve months was estimated as follows:

1996	0	$10,000
1997	0	$10,000

Additional gross profits first year:	$12,500
Future additional gross profits:	
Second year:	$35,000
Third year:	$25,000

This increase in gross profits is as follows:	
Year one:	$12,350
First 18 months:	$27,500
Year one and two:	$47,500

Since June can cancel the newsletter at any time the investment in the technology is limited to the initial $2,500 of her efforts.

This increase in profits (given the Profits Increase Model) would support a technology investment as follows:

2:1 return in 12 months	$6,175 investment
2:1 return in 18 months	$13,750 investment
2:1 return in 24 months	$23,750 investment

Gross profits from June's newsletter investment would justify the $2,500 investment to achieve the targeted 2:1 return within 12 months.

This model allows even the self-employed individual to explore the value of the technology to see if the increases in earnings are enough to justify spending time at whatever value he puts upon his time. The self employed are no different than large corporations and all too often overlook this aspect of developing their technology products.

By utilizing this model, we can explore the value of the technology to see if we expect to increase earnings. As technologists, we all too often overlook this aspect of technology acquisition.

Evaluate Both Business and Technology Risks

Most businesspeople are accustomed to accounting for business risk when they determine return on investment. The business risk concerned in a technology investment is the risk of achieving the desired improvement in the business process without making a difference to customers. Business history shows many examples of "better mouse traps" that don't result in more sales, command a higher price, or achieve greater customer satisfaction. Customers simply don't value the improvement. Sometimes a change accomplishes our desired results, but it doesn't improve business performance. Using our best judgment won't always anticipate customers' reactions. The business process manager is accustomed to these business risks.

I've also learned from experience to watch out for an additional type of risk—technological risk. Such risk usually takes one of two forms. First, it's a risk to bet that a technology will perform in a manner superior to its competing technologies. Even when the implementation cycle is only a few months, sometimes an alternative technology out performs the proposed one before it can be brought online.

A second type of technological risk occurs when a manager commits to a technology, only to find that it doesn't deliver the results originally anticipated. For many of us, the IBM OS2 operating system is a good example of realized technology risk. Customers selected OS2 based on IBM's publicity and advertising. Because OS2 didn't get broad acceptance by PC software developers, OS2 turned out to be an inappropriate operating system for many customers.

Both business and technology risks will always be present. You can't avoid them. If you're aware of these risks, you can plan to make necessary changes if the results of implementation aren't as desired. Technology is changing so quickly that it's a given that you'll make many changes that end in failure. You must acknowledge failure when it occurs. It's best to bite the bullet, terminate the project, and move on to the next project.

Plan for Continual Technological Improvements

Business and technological risks are frightening to undertake. But the risk of doing nothing is even greater. I've always dreamed of running a stable and predictable environment. Unfortunately, from this time forward, a static organizational environment will be impossible to maintain. Today's reality is a world in which business is global and changing rapidly. A manager can't do anything to stop the continual technological improvements. She/he can choose to retire, lead the organization into oblivion, or plan for a steady stream of technological changes to keep information systems improving the business processes.

Today's investment in information technology can only lead to the need for tomorrow's investment in information technology. Technology is creating great value for organizations that understand how to invest in it successfully. As a manager, you should always be looking for and planning the investments that you should be making in your information systems.

DEMAND AN ADEQUATE RETURN FROM YOUR TECHNOLOGICAL INVESTMENTS

With technology changing so quickly, require quick financial returns.

Simple guidelines are okay. For example:

- Cost savings of three times the investment over the twelve- to twenty-four-month period

- Earnings increase of twice the investment over a twelve- to twenty-four-month period

CHAPTER *10*

Technology Investment Management: Showing Return

by Bill Bysinger

"We need $1.5 million to support our computers and people next year."

"Trust me. Our 10% budget increase will barely keep us on our five year schedule to complete existing projects."

"Increase our budget by 20% next year so that we can get all the newest PC stuff."

"All you want is more money and then more money!"

"As a manager I have often created my own monster. Often I have not demanded a return on my technology investments So why should I be surprised when I do not get one."

In this chapter, Bill discusses his change in vision as he shifts from viewing himself as a profit (or cost) center to viewing his technology position as supporting the business manager. He explains how information technology has to show a substantial additional profit or cost saving to the business process. This change in perspective goes a long way toward creating the strong working relationship and assures that technology investments create value for their firm.

Ken Knight

As discussed in the previous chapter, the most important aspect of technology in the 1990s is understanding how to invest in technology and how to leverage that investment. Too often, investment in technology reaps no reward for the company. Normally, no one even talks about return on the technology investment. We typically assume that automation or adding systems will create some major economic benefit almost miraculously.

For the technology manager, competing successfully for funds is paramount in creating an effective information systems environment. I believe that the ability to manage technology investment will ensure, for those technology managers who cultivate it, a highly regarded business career. Those who don't will have short careers. You see, how you manage technology investment is the basic determinant of successful implementations, not the technology itself.

The thought process and actions that lead to successful technology investment begin with this statement: Information systems organizations have no money. That's right. Practically every other division in the company has a mission to create something that will help advance revenues in the company, but not IS. Therefore, the ability to get the money, to secure funding, is the key for IS.

IS IS A SUPPORT/SERVICE FUNCTION

Here we're going beyond zero-base budgeting. This is budgeting based on direct benefit tied to the business. Under this system, the only way to get funded is to do something successfully that will impact someone or some organization in the company other than IS. Information Services has no intrinsic value to the business unless it is directly furthering some other division's ability to increase revenues or significantly reduce costs. IS is not effective in most organizations due to the reverse of this thinking. I've sat in boardrooms and middle-managers' meetings where I was attacked because IS had a bigger budget and more resources than some other operating units. I got tired of this.

Long ago, I decided to change the way I looked at what I did for the company. I stopped trying to be relevant. I quit trying to be a profit center too (although once IS became a profit center when we were split off as a separate, for-profit service bureau for a parent corporation). I realized that I was there to empower others to create competitive advantage. I was a true service. That makes me only as good as my customers' achieved expectations.

Becoming a true service takes a few essential steps and a short time to implement, but a long time to adopt across a corporation. You can show significant results in year one, but adoption across the company requires two or three years in most instances. Here is one example of how I brought about this change in focus.

I was recruited by a high-technology firm to start as director of information systems halfway through the year. When I joined the organization, I inherited a budget that was only a third of what it should have been to make a difference in the business. When I pondered how to solve this financial dilemma, I realized that the only way out was to take a radical approach. I had to convince the business to provide funding to IS in a unique way.

Some of you who are currently senior IS executives may see this as a high-risk scenario. However, I can tell you from my experience that it works. I've used it many times over, very successfully.

Select a High-Impact Project

I decided to look around the business to find out where I could create the greatest impact. I could use IS projects as ways to create the funds I needed to make IS relevant to the business. I spent ninety days talking to everyone in the company who had responsibility for a process that influenced the revenue success of the company. I talked to people in sales, marketing, customer service, technical support, manufacturing, documentation, administration, human resources, and engineering.

What I found was astonishing. I uncovered more than eighty project opportunities that could impact the business in a positive way through the use of technology. However, it wasn't up to me to rank-order the projects—the executive staff made that call. They and their people had made me aware of these opportunities; they should decide which had top priority. In fact, none of these projects had been requested previously through formal channels. I also discovered that many of the projects my IS staff were working on at that time were not really that relevant to the workings of the business. Is this happening in your own shop?

THE MODEL

I decided to create a way for the executives to deal with this prioritization in an existing forum that lends itself to good dialogue—the budget review. I built a project model to set criteria for determining if a project had merit to begin our discussion at all. That model is as follows:

Purpose

All projects must optimize the capital investment, minimize future increases in expense, lower costs associated with nonconformance (quality/productivity measurement), and maximize corporate productivity.

Priorities

Projects will be prioritized based on the following criteria:

1. Cost to develop and implement

2. Return on investment
3. Strategic importance
4. Time to complete

Compliance

- Reduce labor cost increases in areas tied to product delivery and product revenues.
- Reduce labor expense in areas tied to growth and support of the installed base.
- Focus decision support capability to maximize personal productivity at all levels by minimizing redundant tasks, activities, and information.
- Optimize the flow of information across the corporation by providing easy access and timely response.

Decision Process

- Each project will have a one-page brief on what it is, why it is needed, what return it will bring, and how much time and money it will cost.
- Only projects that have potential for the following return on investment (ROI) are considered:
  - Cost reduction: 3:1 in twelve months
  - Profit generation: 2:1 in twelve months

- Each VP gets to vote for the most important projects.
- The executive committee sets the project priorities

Using this model, I put briefs on all eighty of the identified projects in a binder. The projects were divided up by VP area of responsibility. Each project was described in a one-page brief with the following information:

- Project title
- Brief two-line description
- Project sponsor (name, title, and department of highest manager aware of the project)
- First-cut cost estimate at a macro level (including staff, consulting, and technology)
- Estimated ROI calculated, including the formula used
- Two-line articulated benefit

At the bottom of each page were spaces for votes. I told the executives they could cast the following votes:

- Accept this project outright with funding earmarked for approval (final funding would be approved on a definitive cost benefit analysis to follow)
- Postpone for further study
- Approve to a specific funding level
- Kill the project

THE MEETING

I asked for a three-hour meeting with the executives to go over my first budget at the company. I showed up for the meeting with five binders and explained what I was going to do. The executives were surprised but, as I described the process, they became more intrigued.

I told them that my mission was to make the company successful through better technology and information systems. If they wanted me to make the investments in technology, I needed to make sure I was addressing the right issues. As I described the process we would use, it became clear that they were ready to attack it in this way. The meeting also gave them an opportunity to become aware of and discuss their business issues with their peers.

THE RESULTS

The process worked well. I received funding on forty-six projects. The process created the capital I needed to achieve my mission. I used the money on only thirty-eight projects, because of capacity and changes in the business. My budget was increased 2.5 times (rather than the scheduled 15 percent), and I created 3.6 times ROI on this investment for the company in year one.

You can see from this that if you follow your instincts and keep the business focus, you get the funding. You can also understand that each dollar you get needs to be used wisely because it could have been used alternatively to create a new product, expand into a new market, acquire another company, or purchase a technology product to leverage more business.

This model is simple. If someone wants technology to make a difference, the down payment is one-third or half of the ROI. If the business organization will write you a check for the amount, you can guarantee delivery. In my opinion, the best funding model for IS allocates 30 percent of the total IS budget to infrastructure. The remaining 70 percent had better be making a difference in the business and giving back two to three times that 70 percent.

By using this technique in one company, I succeeded in building global, mission-critical client/server systems and technologies. My success wasn't owing to client/server technology. When I started the project, everyone had an unleveraged PC on his or her desktop that wasn't creating opportunity for the company. These investments in PC technology were being underutilized. When I gave them better access and global capability, they created increased revenues for the company. In this case, client/server was the only way to leverage these investments.

This is what technology investment management is all about. I believe IS and technology investments can make a difference, but not through technology alone. We make a difference through wise investments and financial strategies to leverage every nickel we put into technology.

Ask yourself how much of your technology is showing a daily return. This process works. Without this process, you're cheating the company.

TECHNOLOGY INVESTMENT MODELING: The Business Manager and Technologist Agree

Here is a quantitative model that you can use to facilitate decisions on acquiring or building technology. Our investment model must always carry the return on the technology and process investment (ROI). (This is the same model described in Chapter 7 but with different examples.)

ROI = 3:1 on cost savings over twelve months through twenty-four months.

ROI = 2:1 on revenue or earnings increase over twelve months to twenty-four months.

You can use this investment model as a tracking device to justify your investment over time and ensure the return achieved.

What are the main factors to consider in a cost-savings model? First, describe the benefits to the business. For example, if we replace this technology, we will be able to create a better way to process returns. Second, you quantify the savings that you project will be achieved.

Measurements	Current Process	New Process
Cost per hour (average departmental)	$30.00	$30.00
Staff hours (based on 50 weeks):		
Finance	200 hr	
Manufacturing	500	
Customer service	2,350	
Sales	650	
Credit	1,221	
Total	4,921 hr	

New process to reduce by 30% for a new total of 3,445 hr.

	Current Process	New Process
Annual operating costs	$147,630	$103,341
Associated costs:		
Shipping:	$ 29,100 (reduce by 50%)	$ 14,550
Inventory:	106,250 (reduce by 60%)	42,500
Restock costs:	200,000 (reduce by 50%)	100,000
Subtotal:	$335,350	$157,050
MIS costs increased in support: $50,000		
Total costs:	$482,980	$310,391

Savings: $172,589

Total returns processed (current): 9,540

Cost of processing a return: $50.63 $32.53

Projected returns for next year   10,494

Cost of processing returns: $531,311   341,370

Savings: $189,941

This savings using the savings investment model would substantiate the following technology investment:

3:1 return in twelve months $63,314 investment
3:1 return in eighteen months $94,971 investment
3:1 return in twenty-four months $126,628 investment

Each of these investments would need to be closely tracked to substantiate the expected return.

Next, let's look at a model that focuses on the revenue/earnings increase. Too often, we confuse revenue with earnings. Concentrate on earnings.

First, describe the benefits to the business. Getting into a market is time-critical. If we can provide technology to create information that allows us to get to market quicker (or to make a process help get a product to market quicker), such a technology should yield a good business return.

Second, describe the anticipated additional earnings that result from the new technology's allowing the firm to get to market faster.

Measurement	Current Process	New Process
Product time to market	9 months	8 months
Document business requirements:	3 months	2 months
Product pricing	$500	
Projected sales: first year:	5 months	6 months
Units sold	14,000	16,000
Incremental increase:		
First year	2,000 units	
Next six months	4,000	
Total increase	6,000	
OR (broken down by month):		
Projected sales:		
First month	1,000 units	1,000 units
30-90 days	5,000	6,000
90-180 days	9,000	10,000
180 days-1 yr.	24,000	28,000
Total products to market	39,000	45,000

(13 months, due to one month early release)

Revenue generated by increasing delivery to market by one month: 6,000 x $500 = $3,000,000

Margin on the product is 25%, or $750,000

Projected first year sales accelerated based on faster to market = $3,000,000

The earnings from first year justify a $375,000 investment (2:1 in twelve months).

This model shows the value of looking at technology as a way to increase earnings. This is an aspect of technology acquisition that is too often overlooked.

CHAPTER *11*

Innovation to Leverage Technology
by Ken Knight

"My MIS organization and I can create innovation in the company. However, since we cannot justify every dollar of research time, we don't spend enough time on it. I always have to sneak it into the company using guerilla warfare tactics to find it."

"Everyone forgets the old ways we used to do things before we had a network and e-mail across the world."

"I remember the project that really got us turned on was when the Customer Service VP got excited about our new way to deliver desktop links to the mainframe information over the network. That was innovation that showed major dividends in the long run."

MIS executives and their organizations want to be more involved in research and technology to create value in the business. The rapid movement of business and the rapid changes available in technology today can create major competitive advantages in business.

In this chapter Ken emphasizes that the key to innovation is continuous process improvement and applying technologies where it has the greatest need. Most busi-

> ness managers see technology as a way to lower costs, not so—it is a way to leverage change and create new opportunities.
>
> **Bill Bysinger**

History shows us that even the most successful cultures or organizations flourish only for a time. Then, because they're unable to renew themselves, they deteriorate. Cultures of past eras faded after their military might waned—among other causes.

Our society today is driven, to a significant degree, by business organizations. These organizations are very susceptible to failure resulting directly from their past successes. IBM, Sears, General Motors, and Pan American Airlines are a few of the more notable examples of modern firms that ran into difficulties stemming from their past success.

IBM followed a path that led to a dominant position in the mainframe computer business. Then critical technology shifted such that PCs and minicomputers gained clear performance and preference advantages. Even with its world-class technology and technologists in all areas of the computer industry, IBM, hamstrung by its bureaucratic organization, was unable to introduce technology that would support its leadership of the computer industry in the 1990s. New firms introduced new technology that would dramatically reduce the demand for IBM's traditional mainframe computers. These included Digital Equipment in minicomputers, Intel in computers on a chip, and Microsoft in PC operating systems. The innovations of hundreds of other companies shifted the technological advantage from the mainframe market to minicomputers and PCs. Change continues with the shift to computing networks, the Internet, distributed computing, and the World Wide Web.

This was not the first time IBM had lost a dominant market position by failing to adjust to new technologies. A decade earlier, the IBM Selectric typewriter had lost its market position to electronic typewriters, followed quickly by PCs. Within a few years, the IBM Selectric moved from approximately 75 percent of the office typewriter market to less than 25 percent of that market.

HOW TO FAIL: REWARD PROCESSES THAT SUCCEEDED IN THE PAST

Many of today's most successful businesses will fail because they're reproducing their past success. As organizations grow, they become more bureaucratic. Bureaucracy institutes hundreds of rules for how things are to be done in the organization. Some of these rules are written. Many are communicated orally or nonverbally as part of the organization's culture. These bureaucratic rules dictate appropriate employee behavior and influence how employees think. And these rules will largely govern how technology is managed. Bureaucracies remember which ideas didn't work and, therefore, shouldn't be attempted again. Unfortunately, bureaucracies continually use the same solutions to past problems. Bureaucracies depend on the organization's historical successes.

As organizations mature, their own history increasingly controls what they consider appropriate. The bureaucracy rewards employees who avoid making mistakes. Accepted behavior too often becomes "Do nothing." As a result, many of the new technical concepts created in larger organizations are actually commercialized by small or start-up organizations.

About twenty-five years ago, I helped found a company called Creative Publications, Inc. Our product was built on the creative talent of Dale Seymour. Dale had developed supplemental math instructional materials. These included a series of games, posters, graphs, and more for students from kindergarten through high school. Dale had approached many of the major textbook publishers to produce and market the products. They all responded that they didn't publish supplemental math educational materials because they didn't make money. One decade later, these same publishers were calling us anxiously to see if they could acquire our firm.

The history of innovation in the computer industry, both hardware and software, follows this path. New firms are critical to the innovation process, and small or new firms have been the path to commercialization for many technology advances. Digital Equipment Corporation introduced the minicomputers that were overlooked by the mainframe manufacturers. Compac, Inc., created a company based on portables ahead of the established computer manufacturers. Silicon Graphics, Inc., innovated in graphics hardware and software to generate sophisticated graphics capability. Microsoft innovated in PC operating systems. These are a few of the thousands of companies that became large as a result of innovative new information systems technology.

A VICTIM OF ONE'S HISTORY

It's easy to become a victim of one's own history. And nowhere is it more shackling than in the area of technology and technological change. At a time of accelerating technical change, it is critical that managers learn how to make their organizations supportive of appropriate innovation in new technology.

INFORMATION SYSTEMS ARE INTERNAL TO ORGANIZATIONS

In business, we talk about products and services. When it comes to managing information systems, our product, which is technology, is internal to the business. The examples of bureaucracy given earlier refer to products and services sold externally by companies. Unfortunately, bureaucracies have even greater control over internal systems.

Most businesses receive frequent input from the outside world that tells them to pay attention to their products, services, or finances. Their customers let them know when they don't provide the product or service that's expected.

Even if customers don't communicate directly, they vote with their feet and their order forms. Customers' messages are brought to a corporate executive's attention immediately. The company and all those jobs hang on the response.

Similarly, the financial community speaks loudly when the organization's financial performance is lacking. Lender and shareholder expectations and requirements are critical to the company's ability to obtain required capital (and the CEO's ability to keep his or her job).

As CEO, I have yet to encounter a situation where my information system's performance comes under anything like the scrutiny of either my products and services or financial performance. When it comes to our internal information systems, they don't have the same degree of visibility.

Information systems are internal. Their shortcomings don't elicit screams from external constituents. Without customers or financial markets sending quick signals on their product, most senior managers show little concern about the state of their computer and communications information systems. Therefore, it's easy for an executive to ignore what's going on with the firm's computer and communications technology.

CREATE VISIBILITY FOR YOUR IS PERFORMANCE

As the old saying goes, "Out of sight, out of mind." It shouldn't come as a surprise that so many companies haven't developed a mission and objectives statement for their information systems effort. Without the mission and objectives, it's likely that there won't be an evaluation of the information systems' effectiveness. There will be no determination whether or not they're providing desired support for, and enhancement of, the organization's business processes.

Hence, it becomes part of your job as a manager to find ways to make your organization more aware of the state of your information systems. You need to ask if your information systems support your business processes. Further, are your information systems utilizing new technology to enhance the performance of your business processes? And have you reduced your information systems expenditures?

Your job is to keep the organization focused on the quality of your information systems, as well as on your products and services.

THE PEOPLE CLOSEST TO THE BUSINESS PROCESS HAVE THE BEST INFORMATION

To start thinking about ways of utilizing technology to improve the business process, I describe the business process as it crosses the various functional areas of the organization. Our organizations grew up around functional areas. Our information systems followed suit. I confess that I'm guilty of allowing the functional areas to define information systems automated by my computer professionals. At Lex, Creative Publications, and Wm. B. Wilson, I've found functional staff driving the specifications and priorities for systems.

At Creative Publications, our financial people controlled the computer system. As a result, most of the priority applications were financial. Our creative staff became frustrated enough to acquire their own computers with better graphics and publication capabilities.

I shouldn't feel too guilty because such functional tyrannies are fairly typical of corporate life. In my roles as both business school professor or dean and consultant, I wander through some of the largest and smallest corporations in America. I observe that computer applications mirror the requests of functional areas. The functional tyrant rarely looks at needs flowing from the business process as it crosses functional areas. Therefore, I'm not surprised when the computer group is located under the manufacturing function on the organizational chart and manufacturing is served well, while others, like human resources, marketing, finance, research, and customer service, go wanting.

The hardest thing for me to remember is that the people who are close to the business process know what's going on. Remember our project team, which we pulled together to specify our business process? When I brought this cross-functional team together, I discovered an enormous amount of information in the heads of these people.

They're on the firing line. They know what's going on, what's working, and what isn't!

Several factors work against empowering the right people. There's my old temptation to be the one who knows best. Old habits are hard to break. Then there's the corporate bureaucracy, which is hard to overcome—the separate functional groups really don't want to know about our business process. We can all think of reasons why information technology is not very important.

Even so, I have within my own organization the very people who know exactly how our information systems are messed up. They know how bad things are and that they can't get much worse. They do care about the systems because information failures cause them a lot of extra work and rework.

The problem is: These people just don't feel that they can make a difference. They don't believe that anyone listens to them. They don't believe that anyone in senior management really cares.

It's up to me as a manager to figure out how to take advantage of the knowledge of these people close to the business process. I must rethink how I do things. I must overcome the insecurity that prevents me from admitting that I don't have all the answers. I need to trust my employees more. Everything is *not* my responsibility.

INNOVATION IS A NECESSITY

Ignoring the issue isn't an alternative. Technical change is rushing on at a quickening pace. But technology must be introduced with a purpose. We've seen from examples of casual implementation of networked PCs that technology for technology's sake actually creates new problems.

When the obstacles become too confusing, I give myself a pep talk that sounds something like this: There *are* employees who make the business process work. Relax, Ken! Go see your project team. Involve them in describing the business process. Get the business process managers to work with the technologists. Describe the business process. Select the key opportunities where technology should be able to enhance the business.

UTILIZE ALL THE ORGANIZATION'S INFORMATION

The truth will set you free—a simple concept, but a very powerful one. My point here is that the manager directs the project team to go for the truth. Clarify that the team's assignment is to ignore the usual game-playing that acts to avoid issues. The team should be a safe place to share honestly views about areas where we can improve the business process. The project team is in the best position to know what's right and to do what's right. The team knows how the bureaucracy impedes progress, and it knows areas of the business process where technology can make a difference. Such a project team approach is the only long-term solution that I feel will create continuous business process improvement in the organization's information systems.

LEVERAGE TECHNOLOGY, NOT HISTORY

Here are the simple steps to leveraging technology:

1. Highlight the information systems performance in your organization.

    - Identify the impact of IS on the different business processes.

    - Have the management team brainstorm the performance of the IS to identify what works well and where improvement could be helpful.

    - Value the input of the individuals closest to the business process. They have the best information.

2. Information technology solutions of the past often will not be appropriate for today's challenges.

    - The electric highway (networks and webs) change all the ground rules for how businesses operate.

    - All areas of technology are in a state of rapid change.

    - Customer requirements are in a state of rapid change.

3. Look outside the organization for information technology ideas.

    - Technology ideas are everywhere in today's popular media. Read and observe broadly to discover what might help your organization.

- Ask your customers what ideas they have about how technology might help you service them better.

- The generation gap is real. Look to other employees who think differently than peers your own age.

CHAPTER *12*

Products and Measurement: The IS Manager and the Art of Selling by Bill Bysinger

"When I call our help desk they always seem to have just hired a new kid who reads the manual to me over the phone. I call it the helpless desk!"

"Our IS culture is clear; don't ask and don't tell— don't know!"

"My IS people hide in the computer room where I can never find them."

"Why does Jim, the manager of manufacturing computing, always tell me what our manufacturing materials system should look like without even asking any of us what we want?"

I must remind myself continually that it is my responsibility to work with my technologists to help them acquire these critical behavioral and people skills. In most cases, I have been quick to provide opportunities to keep their technical skills honed but have neglected these more elusive interpersonal skills.

Bill revisits the behavioral characteristics that lead to the success of the technologist, which he discussed in

> *Chapter 6. In this chapter, Bill emphasizes that technology alone is not sufficient to assure the success of the technologist. My experiences totally support Bill's beliefs. I find that almost every time I have seen a technologist fail repeatedly, it has been because of his or her inadequacy in the areas of listening, or in the ability to work with other individuals or in a team.*
>
> *Ken Knight*

The greatest challenge for IS directors in the 1990s is to become effective salespeople. I mentioned this point earlier. This chapter will flesh it out.

Most of us IS directors meet with vendor sales people at least once a month and, during the buying cycle, once a week. As an exercise, let's ask ourselves what we like about vendor representatives. Why do we buy from one and show the others out of the office? I've come to conclude that we like the salesperson who listens, tries to understand our business, and can interpret our ideas and frustrations into better ways to use their technology.

In the mid-1980s, I joined a major computer manufacturer as an IS consultant before it was ready for consultants. I was asked if I should reside in the support or the sales division. I chose sales because I wanted to learn what made the vendors who had called on me successful. At sales school, I learned many things about good systems analysis. Yes, that's right, systems analysis. In fact, I wish I could send all my systems analysts to sales school.

SYSTEMS ANALYSTS AS SALESPEOPLE

Why sales school for systems analysts? Let's make an interesting comparison. How often have you purchased a product unsuccessfully? Compare that to how many times you've had to modify systems after delivering them. In sales school, you learn to listen, analyze the situation, determine the need, clarify your understanding, get "buy-in" for your ideas, present a solution, and get closure on acceptance of the solution. If this isn't good requirements definition, solution presentation, and end-user acceptance, I don't know what is. Yes, good salespeople are actually exceptional systems analysts.

Now, what does this have to do with you as an information systems manager? It has everything to do with how you identify strategic opportunities within the business, and how you sell your ideas for solving these critical issues.

We need to look at paralleling sales technique inside the organization. I've used an inside sales technique in the many companies where I managed technology. When I joined one company as their first director of information systems, I used this technique.

The scenario goes something like this. The first three months on the job, I held thirty-five to forty meetings a week. This added up to almost one meeting per hour. Why would I do this?

Listen First

I wanted to find out from the people who managed either processes or people in the company what they needed to be successful. I was actually looking for their "critical success factors," but I don't recommend using this term, which is apt to be unfamiliar to those without an MBA, or Stanford or Big Eight seminar training. Instead, I asked them to specify information they needed, but couldn't obtain, on a daily, weekly, or monthly basis. I also asked questions to find out what they did, why they did it, and what this information would do to improve their work.

Two amazing things happen when you ask such questions. First, you learn a great deal about the managers in the company and their needs. Second, and most important, you take an interest in them. They perceive that, because you listen, you care. I've found this to be the best way to gain acceptance in a company. This approach produces good PR, a lot of learning on your part, and many allies for you from the trenches to the top. I call this the "guerrilla warfare" approach to systems definition.

I learned this tactic from my father. He was a career army officer, a specialist in counterinsurgency (guerrilla warfare). He used to tell me, "Make friends with the natives. They'll give you knowledge, and they'll protect you."

He was right. When I talk to, and listen to, "the masses," the variety of users in companies, I gain a lot of acceptance. The systems I design are also accepted more readily. These users are the real workers. They are the true power base in any progressive organization.

Deliver Product and Services the IS Customer Needs

We've just completed one level of sales technique, called Listen to Your Customers and Understand Their Needs, or Salesmanship 101. To move to the next level, we take this discovered knowledge and turn it into an opportunity. Here we're looking for opportunities to define technologies that will help these users deliver their products or services to market. After I had answers to my questions, I needed to determine what products and services I provided to the company that made a difference meeting the specified needs.

I listed the products of IS:

- Network and system uptime
- Application functionality
- Answers to questions at the help desk
- Terminal or PC repair
- Network bandwidth
- Process analysis
- New technology or system proposals
- Project management
- ROI on a project
- Consulting expertise
- Dial tone
- Information access

- Ease of use
- Security

Then I asked myself: If these are the products, how do we market them? Marketing begins with articulating the benefits of using a product or service. In the most appropriate cases, all services and products provided by IS should help users directly to enhance their missions.

Think about how powerful the effect is when a service or product you provide actually translates into business advantage. Too often, we don't notice the business advantage because technology is so prevalent in business. We forget what its real benefit is. We also forget what the penalty would be if the technology were not present.

Here's an example to consider: the use of global electronic mail. What if a critical project needs input from a remote location? If five time zones separate the sender from the receiver, without electronic mail, the project would depend on slow surface mail or phone systems that may not always be available.

E-mail Saves the Day

In 1991 I was working on a critical-path project between my company's European branch, our U.S. engineering group, and a third-party developer in Poland. I was using electronic mail as my main method of communication. My IS organization had worked with MCI to install and configure a mail gateway between our electronic mail system and MCI. The remote developer in Poland had been experimenting with MCI mail. While our European branch was trying to reach us through local postal services, my mail administrator in the United States intercepted a message to the president of our company on MCI mail link to our electronic mail system. This message saved the project.

This single message not only saved a project but it proved that we could communicate behind the Iron Curtain in a more efficient way. We started to contact developers all over the globe. We did all this using a technology that cost us less than $5,000 to install and configure.

Display IS Accomplishments in Short Graphic Sound Bites

How do you quantify such successes? The best way is to tell the company what you've done for them lately. But don't tell them in long text-based reports. Use highly graphic reports with newsworthy headlines. This kind of report not only points out your successes, but it also highlights how you are doing in uptime, connections, traffic, and response time. Examples of effective reporting techniques follow:

- Provide a bar chart of network uptime by server, LAN segment, WAN connection, or transaction processor.
- Provide trend analysis that highlights issues and resolutions.
- Build a pie chart of help desk activity to highlight problem areas and get better visibility for how the company can help you and how you are helping it.

- Build a global map and show all links, with traffic statistics.

Such detailed reporting is essential. I believe that you'll never get support for your mission if you don't make known the scope of your responsibility and quantify it. I've experienced continual success in obtaining IS funding by making sure that the scope of my responsibilities is well understood and that the mission is framed properly. Recently, in a company where I was the contract CIO, I framed the IS organization by listing all the operating systems, network connections, and processors IS had responsibility for in the company mission. You would have thought I'd opened a treasure chest! All of a sudden, the scope was visible. The users became allies in helping IS achieve its mission. You see, they finally understood the scope of the problem. Such understanding also helped upper management recognize IS resource needs. As a result, management and delivery of IS within the business became much more professional.

Bring IS Out of the Closet

Selling is about positioning, educating, and showing value. For too long, IS has been almost invisible. It's time to let everyone know what you have done lately. You might be surprised by how others will begin to appreciate your issues and, consequently, to take constructive advantage of your products and services.

You need to let the company know what you do that makes a difference. You also need to tell them what new products and services you can bring to the table to make a difference. Remember—promote only technology that has a tangible benefit to the company. If you can't articulate the technology's benefit to your users, you're wasting your time with it. Again, communicate in business terms. Don't talk bits and bytes; talk value and results.

PRODUCTS AND MEASUREMENTS

This is the list of significant products that information systems organizations bring to the business and the tangible measurements that can be applied to each to contribute to the business.

Most information systems organizations do a terrible job of telling the company what they are doing to maintain the business.

Products of Information	*Systems Measurements*
Network and systems	Percentage of available uptime
Application functionality	Define in projects

Products of Information	***Systems Measurements (cont.)***
Help desk calls	Number taken in a specific period of time (Week/month) percentage closed, open, pending
Terminal or PC repair	Numbers addressed
Network bandwidth	Map geography and report on availability
Process analysis	How many accomplished or in process
New technology or systems proposals	How many and projected ROI or business benefits
Project management	Projects in process and what phase (e.g., proposal, approval, requirements, design, coding, testing, implementing)
ROI in projects	Running total of business benefits by month and quarter (revenue generation, profit margin, process improvement)
Consulting expertise	Number of engagements and business units involved

Products of Information	Systems Measurements (cont.)
Dial tone	Number of phones, voice mail boxes, switches, long distance inbound and outbound lines
Information access	Number of databases, database users, database storage
Ease of use	Application and technology surveys
Security	Users, access levels established, monitoring, and breaches (test and nontest caught)

Information systems organizations should publish these statistics on a regular basis to the entire company management.

CHAPTER 13

Creating Heroes: Managing the Technology-Empowered Organization by Ken Knight

"There are days when I feel like MIS is the brunt of all problems in the company. Very few ever say thanks for a job well done. I spend much of my time keeping my staff pumped up and energized."

"Everyone forgets what a good job we did on connecting the entire company, but as soon as one server goes down, you would think the sky is falling."

"I always tell my people, the day we are truly successful is the day the phone stops ringing on the help desk. Response time seems to be the only measure of success."

MIS people do great work for the company under almost battlefield conditions, however very few in the company every say thanks. The thank yous come from the individuals in the front line business who see someone in MIS fix an immediate problem. Rarely do managers and executives ever say thank you, instead they are the first to criticize.

If MIS and business managers can work closer together to solve business problems, they might begin to appreciate the others responsibilities.

> *In this chapter Ken reflects on the need to celebrate successes in information systems and technologies that have been applied to the company. He also stresses the importance of verbal rewards to those involved in the process. There is no better feeling for a business person or a systems person than knowing that they played a role in the success of the company.*
>
> *Bill Bysinger*

Have you ever been in a high-powered, high-achieving organization? I have. It's a fantastic high. I relate it to peak experiences over my lifetime that go back to incidents in my childhood. I remember clearly riding in the wagon my brother and cousin built using old baby carriage wheels. I also recall the applause for our successful drama presentation in elementary school. Another high point occurred when our swim team completed a winning season. The constant factor in these experiences is a great feeling of success.

Peak experiences continued throughout my college years, but as I moved into adulthood, these highs decreased.

PEAK EXPERIENCES IN BUSINESS

Some of my most exhilarating moments have come in the new ventures I've been involved with. For instance, I enjoyed hectic, last-minute shipping sessions for Creative

Publications during our busy August season. I remember the rush of adrenaline at Lex Systems as we worked to get our computerized vehicle-scheduling system out. There was excitement in the air at Eagle Investments as we finished constructing five buildings for the U.S. Forest Service.

I wasn't at Lockheed, but I've read about Kelly's Skunk Works with great interest. To many of us in business, the Skunk Works has been an example of how much a high-powered team can accomplish. The F-80, the U-2, and the Blackbird F-71 are only a few of the concept-breaking airplanes that Kelly's Skunk Works produced.

The same kind of highs happen in many technology companies as they create new products or services. In the Seattle area, we call this the Microsoft culture. This culture is one in which all members of the project team exhibit excitement and enthusiasm. All team members evidence tremendous effort and cooperation. They project a can-do attitude, it is the expectation that the team will accomplish ambitious project goals. The positive outcome is never in question. In such a culture, life is exciting. It's great to be a member of one of these high-powered, high-achievement organizations.

I ask myself a simple question: What creates such organizations? Certainly not the people, I would say from my experience. While I was a professor at the University of Texas at Austin, I was also actively involved in both Creative Publications and Discovery Toys, Inc. These were both high-achievement organizations. The University of Texas at Austin, despite its worldwide reputation, was not a high-achievement organization. This was true, at least, for the College of Business, where I worked.

Clear, Precise Mission and Goals

Several factors at Creative Publications and Discovery Toys led to the creation of high enthusiasm and achievement. Everyone involved in each of these organizations understood the mission. I knew exactly why everything I did made a difference. I knew each day whether my work was excellent or not. I understood the contribution of each person involved in my work group (and everyone in the organization). We cheered each other on every day; we celebrated our team members' successful accomplishments; and we had fun together at work.

WEAK INTERNAL CRY

To understand one barrier to creating a high-power, high-achievement organization in the information systems area, we return to the problem discussed in Chapter 9. I mentioned that the external world tells us when there are problems with our products or our financial performance. Customers tell us when our products aren't meeting their requirements, our quality is inferior, our pricing is out of line, or our service is inadequate to their needs. Financial markets, stock owners, stock analysts, and banks are quick to tell us when our financial performance is unacceptable.

The voices of customers and financial markets are very loud. When they speak, most top managers listen. When they complain, managers act. After all, customers create the organization's viability. The financial markets determine the chief executive's tenure. Messages from financial markets, like those from customers, can't be ignored.

In contrast, information systems customers are primarily internal to almost every organization. When they complain, they speak with a very soft voice. Internal problems don't readily gain top management attention. Senior management doesn't get very worked up over internal complaints. I certainly never worried as much about my information systems shortcomings as I did about external marketing and financial market complaints.

The more bureaucratic the organization becomes, the quieter the internal cry for help. And the more a manager allows a utility mentality in the computer and information systems group, the weaker the internal cry.

The combination of the weak internal cry and the utility mentality causes two characteristics of interest here. First, information systems groups have become relatively isolated. For many reasons, they are removed emotionally and often physically from the key business process of the organization. Second, they receive very little recognition from the rest of the organization, especially top management. The information systems group is seen as either a necessary evil to be tolerated or as a part of the organization that just doesn't seem to know what the organization is about.

A CULTURE WITHOUT HEROES

Unfortunately, these forces generate a culture without heroes. As I discussed earlier, the head of computing or information systems resembles an athletic coach—he or she is highly susceptible to being fired. Top managers need to blame someone for the failure of the computer area, particularly in the utility model, to deliver what the management team thinks they should be receiving. The information systems top dog doesn't even get the acclaim a winning sports coach would. All the IS manager receives is the recognition that he or she didn't let the company down this time. And, most unfortunately, the excitement of a high-performance, high-achievement organization is rarely allowed to spill over into the computer and information systems operations.

To me, this doesn't seem like a very enjoyable environment in which to work. Where's the excitement in an environment where a manager can never really win big but is very likely to be perceived as the goat? This is not an environment that supports high performance and great deeds.

CREATE A HEROES ENVIRONMENT

Throughout this book, I've talked about creating a challenging team situation that includes all the participants involved in the business process. The employees involved would come from the various areas of the organization. This team would work to create solutions to business process problems where computer communications and other technologies can be used to enhance the company's business process. When they find solutions, my job as manager is to celebrate their accomplishments both big and small. When I stop by to see the team, I should either ask them what else they're going to do for me or I should celebrate what they've already accomplished.

CELEBRATE THE INFORMATION SYSTEMS SUCCESSES...

Celebrate their successes wildly. Such celebration is the stuff that makes heroes. Such an environment nourishes and builds high-performance, high-achievement teams. You produce a can-do attitude of openness and honesty, which leads to the business process successes you desire. You need to celebrate both activity and trials. This means that you celebrate the team's attempts to create business process improvement. Your role is to let the team know that what they're doing is important and that what they're creating will make a real difference to the organization. Specifically, you can tell them exactly what that difference will be.

It's important to stop by the team's work area so that they know they're important to you and the organization. Thank them for what they're doing. Thank them for their cooperative effort. Thank them for working to understand each other. Offer them support if they need it.

...AND

Celebrating the success of the project team is the easy part. For me, the much more difficult task is celebrating their failures. I've found that failures will occur whenever I work on technology implementation. Creating technological change is entering the zone of the unknown. *Not everything will work.* I must admit that at all times. I'll say that again: Not everything will work. In fact, an at least partial failure is more likely than a complete success. I learn more from my failures than I do from my successes, but it is often hard for me to make the best use of failures, because I don't easily admit to mistakes. After all, I'm supposed to be a successful manager!

I was talking the other day to a vice president of a large insurance company whose entire job is to bring about change in that organization. She said that change in middle management is the hardest to bring about. The company is moving away from business functions that once had twenty human steps, each of which could have taken several days to process. This meant that processing insurance applications, adjustment claims, and litigation issues could easily take weeks to complete. They now want the individual closest to the business process, the customer, to carry out the entire process alone in a matter of several hours with computer. This creates enormous savings in the cost to complete the task, that is, overhead. As she talked with me, she emphasized the difficulty the middle managers had in dealing with change. They remember the old days; when a mistake was made and an error occurred, the "responsible individual" was fired. She said that "a manager must reward 100 individuals for attempting and creating a change to offset punishing only one guilty."

Celebrating failures is what is necessary if we are to address the reluctance of middle management to embrace change. They know that they must change, but they have a long memory of what happened in the past when something didn't work out.

Recently, I implemented a client/server environment at the Seattle Pacific University School of Business and Economics. Students were running this relatively modest task, which sounded quite easy at first. Well, we found out that the building wasn't wired correctly; the university didn't have enough Internet addresses for the entire faculty and staff; and our planned budget and student resource pool were inadequate. In other words, the implementation didn't go as smoothly as anticipated. So, is this project a success. Not completely! Do I call it a failure?

How I react to a situation like this is critical to the project. I can revert to my old self and, after hearing a brief explanation of the problem, I can find someone to blame. After all, the project was a failure, and there must be someone at fault. I can attack the diligent students who put their hearts into the project. I can try to call it someone else's fault, except that I was the key decision maker. I set the scope of the project. I approved the resources allocated to the project. I can ignore the problem and grumble about incompetence and all the problems computers cause. Then again, I can own up to not spending the time to get involved and scope the project objectives and resources adequately. I can recognize that the team made a good start and encourage them to go on from there to complete the job.

Today, I choose the latter route. I celebrate the students' efforts. They took on too big a project armed with too few resources. Given what they had to work with, they took major steps toward accomplishing something that the School of Business and Economics really needs. Without knowing that their task couldn't be done, they accomplished a great deal. They deserve to be treated as heroes.

They are in a high-performance, high-achievement mode. As I treat them like heroes, they charge on to accomplish what each of us now realizes is needed. True, we aren't doing what I had originally expected, and the process takes a little more time than I had thought it would. But I must realize that what I had originally expected was unreasonable. The team did far more than I should have expected, given the resources I provided. They did so with excitement and enthusiasm. They deserve to be treated as heroes. The next iteration is likely to bring the results I expected, results I had so poorly specified in my initial request.

DEVELOP THAT CAN-DO ATTITUDE

At the next iteration, I hired Michael, one of the students who had volunteered for the project, to continue the implementation of the server system. I watched with interest as Michael proceeded with the project. He wasn't an expert. Because he knew that he didn't have all the knowledge to accomplish the project, he asked the faculty and staff what they needed and what their problems were.

The next thing I heard was that faculty and staff were excited about what Michael was doing for them. From the outset, Michael was dealing with more than just server problems. He helped them install and set up new programs on their computers. He helped them get their nonfunctioning printers to work. Michael also specified equipment enhancements needed to run their special software. He dealt with all sorts of problems that faculty and staff were experiencing with computing and information technology. When the possibility arose that Michael might not continue working for SBE, faculty and staff immediately told me about all he was doing to solve their day-to-day problems. Michael helped them function more effectively and efficiently. Since Michael didn't know the answer to every question, his practice was to listen to the individual user's problem and then go back to his work area to learn how to solve that problem. He considered no question too difficult or too dumb. Michael took the position that he could find the answer by reading about it or by asking those with more information. And that is exactly what he did.

When I talked to the faculty and staff—more than forty of them—whom Michael had helped, they raved about all he was doing for them. They felt that he was accomplishing a lot. It was very clear to me that Michael was a hero.

Contrasting Reactions

During this time, I had an opportunity to talk to the person who managed university-wide information systems activities. His reaction to Michael stemmed from his viewpoint as a computer information systems expert. He said that "Michael was playing with only half a deck," meaning that Michael didn't have all the technical knowledge needed to respond quickly to all the requests that were made of him. The computer manager went on to say, "Michael is a very bright and helpful undergraduate student. But, for many of the problems or questions given to him, he doesn't know the answer and has to go and find it. He does so in a very helpful way, but he should just know a lot more than he does. He's continually learning on the job."

I feel differently about this. It is exactly Michael's ability to listen to users and fully understand their questions first that has made him a hero in the eyes of the faculty and staff. He doesn't feel that he needs to be an all-knowing expert. He doesn't feel that it is a sign of failure to say, "I don't know, but I'll find out for you." His can-do attitude endears him to his customers. He doesn't respond with an attitude that says "I know what's best for you." He works hard to completely understand the user's need. Only then does he respond with a solution. Even then, he communicates carefully with the user to make sure the solution is actually appropriate. This is the stuff heroes are made of.

The university's technology director is very well-meaning. He wants experts to make sure that everything is done correctly the first time. Unfortunately, in today's rapidly changing world, the problems the process manager faces change quickly. The technology that can be applied to enhance a business process is changing at an explosive rate. Even the experts will frequently find themselves in situations where they are working with "only half a deck." By the way, Michael kept his job until he finished his degree.

Heroes have a can-do attitude. They listen carefully to their business process counterparts. They know that they will have to expand their technical knowledge continually. They are willing to prototype, and then work with the user to make needed improvements. They will celebrate together with their customers as they continually improve the users' systems.

BUSINESS MANAGER AND TECHNOLOGIST CELEBRATE TOGETHER

It is best when business managers and technologists celebrate together. Managers empower the team to create improvement in the business process. The first step, of course, is to have them get started. They may not have all the resources or knowledge they need. Most typically, they probably don't know that they don't have the ability to accomplish the full task. The first iteration is a prototype. The team sees the problem to be addressed and gets started on it. They do what they can to accomplish a good first step. The next few steps will be a lot easier once the first step has been completed. They can celebrate together what they accomplish together. Then the team can go back to work on those tasks that still need to be done with a high degree of excitement. This is the excitement of heroes. The team begins to climb increasing levels of success. We all feel good about each other, what we've accomplished, and what we will accomplish. Along the way, we enjoy working together.

WE FORGET TO CELEBRATE OUR ACCOMPLISHMENTS

We are a society of the covetous; our theme is "I want, I want, I want." We celebrate the sports or music successes of youth. But why does the flow of encouragement slow down after the age sixteen or eighteen? I don't have an answer to that question. But what I do know is that most of today's organizations have forgotten to celebrate the everyday successes and efforts we achieve.

It's not difficult for a manager to overcome this shortcoming. Like starting an information systems project, your job as a manager is to just do it. Celebrate with those around you. The great thing for me is that it makes my job more fun! Life is much easier, and I sleep better at night.

Challenge, empower, and celebrate the work of your project team to create the technology that advances your business processes. This will lead your organization to success faster than anything else that I've found.

LET'S CELEBRATE!

Build relationships that show you care. Build a culture that says "We value you." Build an organization with a can-do attitude.

You build such a culture by honoring the people you work with as individuals. This requires a conscious effort. It requires that, in your heart, you seek to understand and do those things that say "I value you, not only for what you do for this organization but for you as a unique person." (Keep in mind that if encouragement is not backed up by the company's incentives program, your words may have a hollow ring.) Here are ways to get started. Not only is it easy to do, but it's fun. Working in an organization that creates heroes allows all of us to be heroes.

Simple steps that allows us to celebrate each other are:

1. Everyday small enabling actions:
   - Comments showing recognition of a person in front of the other workers
   - Saying thanks right at the time it is earned
   - A note of appreciation
   - A card on special occasions, such as a birthday or anniversary with the company

2. Showing concern about coworkers' lives through everyday discussions about what is important to them:
   - A chat over coffee about interests or family, as appropriate

- Conversations over lunch about future plans
- A Saturday outing that explores interests outside the work organization

3. Awards to provide public recognition through company and local newspapers, awards events and luncheons, company web, and so forth:

- Best unsuccessful attempt of the month to be shared within your team (or any time period—a week, a quarter, a year, a day)
- Most significant idea/innovation of the year (or any other time period)
- Cash reward for a contribution to increased profits or cost savings

Not only our celebrating, but our compensation increases and promotions must support heroes. All too often, a culture gives lip service to heroes, but does not reward them with promotions and salary increases. Celebrations will soon ring hollow if there isn't an alignment between the critical organizational rewards and the accomplishments celebrated.

CHAPTER 14

Creating Heroes: Allies in Business

by Bill Bysinger

"We're on our fifth Chief Information Officer in four years. The Board of Directors fires them just when they begin to understand the true complexity of our organization."

"We are now talking rewarding risk taking at the senior management level. The troops still do not believe us and so it is business as usual—don't make a mistake; don't take any risks!"

"It is always someone else's fault when my IS group announce another one-month delay in delivery of my personnel tracking system."

"Must we always shoot the messenger??!!"

Many of the technologists that I have dealt with are skittish when it comes to taking responsibility for their actions or admitting a mistake. Because we lack the understanding of what is going on, we have created this problem by being quick to blame and execute IS professionals for "failures" that occur because of the complexity of the technology solutions that we are requesting.

> *Bill carries my discussion of creating and celebrating heroes to the technologists. Our work needs to be a place in which we enjoy being involved. As I have an opportunity to observe many of today's workplaces, I am continually struck by how dreary and negative so many of them are. No wonder heroes are not created in these cultures. Bill suggests to the information technologists'; in their language, amazingly simple steps that can create a culture of heroes. This is a culture in which I want to work. Developing this culture also represents the best business practice that I know of to create the most value from our information systems.*
>
> **Ken Knight**

Now, let's look at creating heroes from the IS manager's viewpoint. The most rewarding part of my job as a manager of information systems organizations over the past fifteen-plus years has been to create opportunities for technology to make winners out of people in business. The ability to make a difference in the business life of an organization or of a person is what allows "evangelists" like me to believe that technology can be of real value to business and productivity—and that technology can be simple.

These aspects of technology were evident in a situation I encountered in the late 1980s. I was the director of information systems for a technology company. One day, I was hanging around in the customer service area. I happened to watch a service representative using a desktop tool that intrigued me. The service rep was responding to a customer call by zooming through what she called the

HyperManual. She answered my questions by explaining that it was a quick reference guide. HyperManual was built in Hypertext, with high graphics and point-and-click response. This tool allowed sales reps to be efficient with information for their customers.

Naturally, I asked where she obtained this software. She said, "The SPOE developed it." "The what?" I inquired. "The SPOE," she replied. "What is an SPOE?" I asked. And here's what I found out: The SPOE was an underground development group. They met during business hours, normally over lunch, to discuss which productivity tools they could build to help members of their department be more productive. I asked when they met next and decided to show up at their meeting.

When I dropped in, they may have thought that this new IS executive was there to kill the SPOE. Maybe I was concerned about computer hacking in the company. Instead, I asked to listen. I asked to hear their views of the company's systems and how technology should be built and deployed. I was most curious about what they did to develop such useful tools for their departments.

I couldn't help asking how they came up with a name like SPOE. They said it was simple and summed up their mission. The SPOE was the Society for the Paperless Office Environment.

These guys were on a mission to make technology work the way users worked or needed to work. Talk about revelation—this was it! I had found a pocket of innovation in the company that others had ignored. Here was a group in the trenches who believed nothing was impossible. I had found a team that worked nights and weekends delivering technology tools to enhance the desktop lives of users on the front lines of the business.

The SPOE was what I had always wanted IS to be: innovative, driven, focused, fun, excited, and committed to making users successful through technology. The day I met SPOE was a watershed for me. I had found the spark I needed to create a new vision of systems at my company. SPOE was a group of untainted technologists who were ready to respond to the battle call to make systems different. That day, I saw evidence that I could take a traditional, top-down-structured IS model and turn it into a lean and mean client/server network computing model.

GET THE REAL DOERS INVOLVED

I began to get the real innovators involved in the processes of developing and delivering technology. The users were more than ready to take on responsibility for creating systems, and I was going to give them the opportunity.

Things started happening. My IS organization started going out to the users. I killed all projects that were going to take longer than ninety days. I started asking the business managers and our internal IS customers what they really needed. I found projects that I could get users to fund. I found users who were ready to get involved. I also found skeptics who sat back and watched, waiting for me to fail. But the result was that we (not I) succeeded in changing the culture of how to build systems.

Since we didn't have a road map, we made one. We had failures, but we turned them into learning experiences that created further success.

I challenged my IS group with monthly meetings called Futures Meetings. These were three- to four-hour sessions in which we left the status quo behind and allowed each other to be creative and innovative. We brought our wild and risky ideas about how we could improve, create better technology, and paint the future.

I found that those who were turned on by our "nothing is impossible" attitude were the doers in the company—the people who performed the work and could really be productive with better tools and systems. These were the people for whom I most wanted to make a difference. We in SPOE saw the world of these doers as the point where the rubber of our ideas met the road.

We painted an architecture and named it "knowledge technology." Knowledge technology was technology that could anticipate what users needed before they asked for it. We began to look at our global systems. Everything we did was driven by innovation and imagination. The proof of the pudding came when I was presented an award in front of the whole company for being part of the SPOE.

You see, the SPOE and I created many systems together. Some were small and not very significant. The large systems were the ones that made believers of the skeptics, but all of them gave me a great deal of satisfaction. I had always wanted to have fun developing systems. After joining with the SPOE, my outlook changed, not only on how users could use technology that would provide them superior functionality, but also on how we could have fun in the process.

GET PEOPLE INVOLVED—GET THEM TO DO IT!

As a result of this experience with SPOE, the way I manage IS organizations changed. I began to give my IS people freedom to be creative. I encouraged learning, experimentation, and innovation.

Even more important, the SPOE experience affected how the company viewed IS. A specific experience illustrates this change in company thinking. Remember, I was responsible for global IS in a high-technology corporation. At our senior management retreat, a task force presented an intriguing report. This task force had spent the previous quarter looking for pockets of innovation throughout the company and around the world. They had interviewed many people. In the end, they had compiled a list of the most innovative groups in our company.

I remember sitting in the retreat room listening to the task force. They described the methodology they used. They stressed that innovation was critical to our company's success and that it was gratifying to see real innovations happening in some groups in the company. They had compiled a list of innovators. Their list had been kept confidential until this retreat, where our senior managers and executives from around the world sat around in one room. When the moment arrived to unveil the list, I remember thinking, "I hope engineering can prove real innovation is happening for the products' sake."

The team revealed that the top organization for innovation was IS—my group! Boy, was I surprised! Just a year before, we had been considered out of control, too radical in our approach, and sure to fail. Yes, in our high-technology company, where engineering normally reigns supreme, information systems was singled out as the most innovative group in the corporation.

I couldn't have been prouder. I had built my team with people who were considered by many—even by human resources—to have no value or experience. This group of rebels had been quietly building successful global client/server before many others in the world. They were finally recognized by their peers. I was so turned on by this recognition, I couldn't wait to tell the team that they were appreciated and respected for their ability to make a difference.

RISK SHARING ALLOWS FOR FAILURES AS YOU DO IT

You see, it doesn't take years of experience and loads of degrees, or directives from the top, to be successful and do heroic things in IS. It takes a management philosophy that allows people to fail as well as succeed, which also requires guts. It takes encouraging your people. It takes believing that they have more good ideas than you do. It also takes the smarts to believe that they can and should know more than you. My philosophy is to make all those who work for me succeed and give them opportunities to grow. As a result, I will succeed.

I want risk takers around me. I want innovators in my camp. I want people who challenge me. I want a team that plays together, argues constructively, and doesn't believe that anything is impossible. I want to make winners, heroes, and believers of all business users of technology and all technologists who cross my path.

If I do nothing else in my life, I want to make sure that I did something to help people be productive and have fun in the process of using technology. All of us are here to make a difference. Information systems managers are in a unique position to make it happen.

CREATING HEROES: QUESTIONS FOR GAINING ALLIES

Listen and observe the business

1. Where are the pockets of opportunity in the business?

   Look for processes to improve or users to enhance.

2. Who are the desktop users who have built some interesting productivity tools or processes?

   Find the creative people in the business who have used their PCs with creativity.

3. Is there an opportunity to help these users or groups through technology?

   Most organizations and processes could be enhanced through better use of systems.

4. How can I let them take part in the project to improve their process?

    Observe opportunities and let them become ways to improve the business.

5. How do I gain collaboration from the business managers?

    Listen to them and let their people be involved in the process.

6. How can I incorporate the training from the business into systems implementations (quality or process improvement training)?

    Be the only organization that actually uses the business training delivered in its processes.

7. How can I create opportunities for people in the business who may be potential information systems personnel who could bring business knowledge to the business?

    They understand the business and (many times) feel more comfortable with desktop technologies than traditional IS personnel.

8. How can I identify PC users who could be part of my development staff?

    Some of the best new development and desktop support people come from the business.

Farming opportunities in the business creates both heroes and allies that will help IS justify all the capital used to build and extend systems.

CHAPTER *15*

Making It Simple: Integrating Business Management with Technology

by Bill Bysinger and Ken Knight

"I am amazed how easy it was to successfully deliver that complex project. I credit the VP of Sales and Service for making it a success. He really committed the resources, helped me and my organization understand his objectives and goals, and worked as a team with me."

"As I spent time with my Information Systems group I came to understand their problems, and they came to appreciate what information manufacturing needed. What a great success we created together. I was always afraid to get involved. When I did we all got excited and the IS people went "all out" to install my manufacturing system on time and within budget. A first!"

When MIS and Business organizations work together, nothing is impossible: Dates get met, budgets get made, and systems truly contribute to the business.

This is where we have tried to create a partnership between the business and the information systems. Together, these two executives formed a single mission

212 Investing in Information Technology

> *"Create a better more competitive organization through the thoughtful application of technology and information." The results can be dramatic and the value to the business will be a force that excites the people involved and creates new opportunities for innovation and productivity.*
>
> ***Ken and Bill***

We've arrived at the final chapter of this book. While this chapter wraps up all the material presented in the book, we find it enables readers to go on to realize their own missions. In other words, the end of this book, is just the beginning of your journey.

In both business and technology, much is left to be interpreted by the culture in which the methods will be applied. Our methodology must also be applied within business cultures. Early in this book, we posed questions about gaining return on the technology dollars you spend, enhancing productivity via intelligent use of technology, the ability of the IS manager and the business manager to collaborate, and how to survive the rapid changes in technology and business into the next century.

There are no easy answers. Rather than answer every question, we presented some techniques to help make your journey less bumpy. Now it's time to consider those things said (and some unsaid) in this book. Here are some concepts to ponder as you continue your journey:

1. Failures are OK in the process of applying technology as long as we learn from them and internalize what has been learned.

2. Process reengineering is essential, but it must be simple. Take reengineering steps one process or organization at a time. Deliver some regeneration of the process (process improvement) quickly. Remember the ninety-day cycle.

3. It must be acceptable for people in the organization to deliver bad news. Nothing must be sacred—all existing processes and methods must be up for examination. Realism about when things can be done must be encouraged. But, if we take smaller bites in shorter time frames, big changes can happen.

4. Make everything simple. Simplicity must be the battle call for businesses in the 1990s and beyond. When things are too complex, nothing happens, or whatever happens takes too long, and usually success is not measurable.

5. Eliminate the complexity. Everyone should know, in simple terms, the company mission and how it relates to the corporate value delivered to the market. Technology should create simplicity, not complexity, in process.

Remember, Federal Express won the Malcolm Baldridge Quality Award not because it was doing things extremely well, but because a station manager in a remote location could explain the mission and how he fit into it in simple terms.

6. The agenda = the right things, done correctly

Team:

- Business managers: must be able to ask the right questions
- IS managers: must be able to provide business justification for technology in answer to the business managers' questions
- Both must cooperate

Risk:

- Must be taken to accomplish anything
- Must be shared by both the business managers and the IS managers

Managers:

- Must be measured effectively and monitored constantly
- Must be minimized but will never be eliminated

Innovation:

- Must be identified
- Must be encouraged
- Must be rewarded
- Must be fostered via:
    - mentoring by senior management
    - allowing for innovation in the culture of the business
    - holding innovation dear as a cornerstone of a business' intelligent growth

- Must be owned by the people in the business.

This agenda creates value to the business; encourages humility in the way projects and ideas are fostered for success; keeps business and technology synchronized; and creates a world-class approach to solving problems through the application of technology.

Virtual corporations are emerging. Exceptions have become the rule. There are no guidelines. Nor are there barriers to entry to global markets. Technology and information level the playing field.

Technology and information must be enablers. If not, all capital invested in technology is wasted. If you take anything away after reading our book, we hope it is this: Make it simple and make it right.

Technology alone has no value. For a successful partnership between technology and business, neither stands alone. Each must contribute to the other to deliver the desired return and success, as we become the organizations of the future.

KEYS TO INTEGRATING BUSINESS AND INFORMATION TECHNOLOGIES

Following are a list of things to keep in mind as you navigate the minefield of business and information technology integration.

1. Failures are OK; just learn from them.
2. Process reengineering is essential but must be simple.

3. Bad news is OK; everything must be challenged.

4. Make everything simple.

5. Eliminate complexity from the business.

6. Teaming = business and information systems.

7. Risk must be taken, shared, measured, minimized, and cannot be eliminated.

8. Innovation must be identified, encouraged, rewarded, fostered, and held dear.

9. Technology and systems must bring value.

Finally, remember:

- Information systems organizations have *no money*; they just borrow from the business.

- Technology and systems have no value without being applied to the business and creating benefit and tangible return (revenue, profit, and opportunity).

Simplicity and cooperation make successful businesses. We wish you well on your journey.

Bill and Ken

Index

A

aerospace manufacturing, 133
agenda, 213, 215
application software
    See software
"as is" processes, 64–70
    See also process mapping
automobile dealership, 138–140

B

bad news, 213, 216
Ballmer, Steve, 78
bar chart
    for business value, 81
    of network uptime, 179
Black & Decker, 43
Boeing, 33, 43
budget
    decided behind closed doors, 86–89
    measurements, 81
bureaucracy, 163–164, 169, 170, 189
business language, 74–79
business process
    See also project management
    analysis, 58–68
    continual process improvement, 100–101
    costs, 125–126
    defining, 90–91, 94–96
    description, 94–95
    improving, 167–169, 191
    information systems (IS) support, 31–34, 73–74
    managing project teams, 93–94
    methodology, 114–115
    owners, 5–7
    teamwork and, 41–44
    virtual organizations, 38–39, 215
business risks, 143–145
business value, 81, 216

C

can-do attitude, 194–197, 199
celebrating accomplishments, 188, 191–193, 198–200
checklists
    integrating business and information technology, 215–216
    pioneering for customers, 21–23
chief information officer (CIO), 3
client/server technology, 85–89, 155, 207
communication
    in assessing new information technology, 123–124
    barriers to, 93–94
    in project management methodology, 92, 101–103
communication tools, 80
communications technology
    management focus on, 166
    quick payback on, 126–127
Compac, Inc., 164
complexity, 213, 216
computer downtime, 4
computer literacy, 3, 5
computer technology
    See also information systems (IS); information technology (IT); technology investment modeling
    as an investment, 121
    budget considerations, xv–xvi, 119, 121–122

217

challenges, 26, 27–29
creating business advantages, 29–34
electronic communications, 37, 38
innovation, 164–165
management responsibility, 7–8
needs assessment, xiv, xvi
problems, 3, 107
shortcomings, 32
strategic decisions, xx
training, 120–121
computer viruses, 5
continual technological improvements, 143
continuous improvement process, 91–92, 100–101, 102–103
corporate bureaucracy, 163–164, 169, 170, 189
corporate culture, 187–200
cost overruns, 88–89
cost-benefit example, 54, 111
cost-savings model, 156–159
"could-be" process, 66, 69, 71
Creative Publications, Inc.
  celebrating accomplishments, 188
  computer system, 168
  customer database, 124
  innovation, 164
  last-minute shipping sessions, 186–187
creativity, 95, 208
cross-functional teams, 168
customer service, 30, 46
customers
  See also external customers; internal customers
  business managers as, 6, 8–9
  expectations of, 165
  feedback, 188–189
  identifying, 19
  pioneering for, 21–23
customer-shared-risk projects, 18–21

D

Dale Carnegie course, 108
Data Communications, *Tales from the Crypt,* 86–89
Digital Equipment Corporation (DEC)
  minicomputers, 162, 164
  VAX system, 14
Discovery Toys, Inc., 187, 188
downtime, 4

E

Eagle Investments, 187
electronic communications, 37
e-mail (electronic mail), 178–179
evangelism, 106, 109
external customers, 12, 15–18, 66
  See also customers

F

failure
  acknowledging, 102
  celebrating, 192, 193
  learning from, 213, 215
  risk sharing and, 207–208
Federal Express
  computerized information system, 29
  Malcolm Baldrige Quality Award, 213
  team efforts, 43
financial information systems, 113
fiscal responsibility, 81
Ford Taurus, 42
front-line workers, 6
funding (budget), 78
future technology, 109–110
Futures Meetings, 205

G

global map, 180
global systems, 205
"guerilla warfare" approach, 176

H

hackers, 5
Hallmark, 79
head count, reducing, 113–114
heroes environment
  celebrating, 199–200
  creating, 190–191, 202–204
  gaining allies, 208–209
high-achievement organizations, 185–188
human resources
  See also resources
  reducing head count, 113–114
  staff percentages, 82
HyperManual, 203

I

IBM Corporation
  critical technology shift, 162–163
  IBM 650 computer, xiii, xiv
  Selectric typewriter, 163
industry-specific technology, 78
information flow
  in business process analysis, 59, 60
  future design, 69–70
  in process mapping, 64–65
  reviewing process improvements, 71
  visualizing solutions, 66–68
information highway, 9–10
information officers, 120
information systems (IS)
  See also computer technology;
        information technology (IT)
  barriers to achievement, 188–189
  budget, 121–122
  business advantages, 29–31
  in the business process, 31–34, 73–74,
        114–115
  celebrating successes, 191–192
  communication tools, 80
  continual process improvement,
        100–101
  culture, 190
  customer service, 46
  defining mission and objectives, 75–77
  displaying accomplishments in graphic
        sound bites, 179–181
  financial aspects of, 77
  high-impact projects, 150–155
  implementing technology, 7, 83–85
  innovation, 206–207
  internal, 165–166
  iteration process, 98–99
  management, xix, 174
  methodology, 109–115
  in missionary organizations, 36–37
  mission-critical, 8, 86
  perceptions of, 13–14, 16
  products of, 177–178, 181–183
  quality of, 167, 171
  responsibilities, 19–20, 179–180
  scoping projects, 112, 180
  service-based, 149–150
  value, 216

information technology (IT)
  See also computer technology;
        technology investment modeling
  integrating with business management,
        212–216
  leveraging, 171–172
  metal fabricator scenario, 34–36
  responsibility, 110
  returns from investment, 113–115
  strategic technical advantages, 44, 125
  value, 216
  virtual organization created with, 38,
        215
innovation
  in the computer industry, 164–165
  encouraging, 204–205, 206–207
  influenced by technical change,
        169–170
  techniques, 214–215, 216
insurance claim process, 62–63, 68
integrated manufacturing system, 133
Intel chips, 162–163
internal customers, 12, 17, 66, 189
  See also customers
Internet browsers, 39
intranet, 40
intrapreneuring, 106, 114
Iron Curtain, 179
iteration process, 98–99

J

jargon, 94

K

Kenworth trucks, 33

L

labor costs, 152
LAN (Local Area Network), 87–89
Lands' End, 79
legacy systems, 40–41, 100, 133
  See also information systems (IS)
Lex Systems, 6, 187
Lindstrom, Dave, 135–137
listening skills, 176
L.L. Bean, 30–31
Lockheed, 187
low return on investments, 124

220   *Investing in Information Technology*

M

Macintosh computers, 107–108
   See also computer technology
macro processes, 61
"make it simple" (MIS) philosophy, 5, 10
Malcolm Baldrige Quality Award, 213
management
   budget responsibility, 121–122
   creating heroes, 202–209
   critical information, 102
   as the customer, 8–9
   empowering teams to improve business processes, 197–198
   historical perspectives, 163–165
   information officers, 120
   integrating with information technology, 212–216
   owning business processes, 5–7, 34
   passion, 106, 107–109
   responsibility for technology, 7–8, 188–189
   rewarding successes, 192–193
   strategic technical advantages, 44
   styles, xvii
   success factors, 14, 112, 174
   techniques, 198–200
   in the twenty-first century, 10, 212
   utility mentality, 189
manufacturing systems, 113
market, 78
marketing skills, 178
MCI mail, 178–179
measurable objectives, 97
measuring performance, 76, 181–183
meetings, 175
methodology, 109
   See also business process; information systems (IS); project management
micro processes, 66
Microsoft Corporation
   culture, 187
   industry-specific technology, 78
   network system, 87
   PC operating systems, 163, 165
MIS (management information system)
   development to maintenance ratio, 56
   "make it simple" philosophy, 5, 10

   priorities, 46–47
   project delivery time, 51–56
   in the twenty-first century, 10, 212
mission statement, 75–76, 80, 154
missionary organizations, 36–37
mortgage broker, 141–143

N

newsletter publishing, 141–143
NEXT Computer, 79
Nordstrom, 79

O

objectives
   defining, 76–77
   specifying resources, 97
object-oriented programming, 126
ontime project delivery, 51–56
organizational structure, 58

P

Paccar (manufacturer of Kenworth trucks), 33
PC-based systems, 29, 107–108
   See also computer technology
peak experiences, 186–187
pep talk, 170
performance
   improving, 67, 71
   measuring, 78
   monitoring, 76
personal productivity, 152
pie chart
   for budget measurements, 81
   of help desk activity, 179
pie-in-the-sky proposal, 84–85
presentation skills, 106, 107, 109
process mapping, 61–71
process modeling, 110–111
process reengineering, 213, 215
profitability, 78
programming
   languages, xix
   productivity improvements, 126–127
project management
   See also project schedules
   business process models and, 111

communication, 92, 101–103
continuous improvement process,
    91–92, 100–101, 102–103
defining business processes, 90–91,
    94–96
failure, 102
limiting technology implementation,
    91, 96–97
model, 49–51
open communication, 82–94, 89–90
priorities, 47–49
prototype implementation, 91, 98–99
software, 48
success factors, 112
project model, 20
project schedules, 46
    See also project management
project team
    celebrating, 191–192, 198–200
    clarifying assignment of, 170
    creating, 93–94
    techniques, 214, 216
prototyping
    disruption of business process during,
        125
    implementation, 91, 98–99
    modification, 91, 99
public speaking, 109
purchase order process, 69–70

Q

quantifying additional profits, 139–140,
    142–143
quantifying cost savings, 134–135,
    136–137, 156–159
quantitative model, technology investment
    modeling, 156–159
Quayle, Dan, 26
QuickBooks system, 135–137

R

realism, 213
requirements prioritization, 53–54, 55
resources
    defining, 97
    in project management, 48, 50
results reporting, 81–82

return on investment (ROI)
    demanding in technology, 125–126,
        146
    financial return on, 132, 138
    guidelines, 146
    model, 20, 78
    potential, 152–153
    results, 154–155
risk sharing, 207–208, 214

S

sales systems, 113
salespeople, 174, 175
schedules, 46
School of Business and Economics, Seattle
    Pacific University, 85, 193, 194
scope, in project management
    defining, 48, 49, 50
    difficulty with, 112
    limiting technology implementation,
        91, 96–97
Seattle Pacific University, 33, 85, 193, 194
security, computer viruses, 5
self-employed professionals, 143
service systems, 113
Seymour, Dale, 164
Silicon Graphics, Inc., 164–165
simplicity, 213, 216
Skunk Works, 187
Society for Information Management (SIM),
    111
Society for the Paperless Office
    Environment (SPOE), 203–204,
    205, 206
software
    performance, 126
    project management, 48
    SPOE, 203–204
    versioning, 50
sound bites, for IS accomplishments,
    179–176
Southwest Airlines, 4, 86
Stanford University, xiii
success
    celebrating, 191–192
    contributing factors, 14, 174
    in project management, 112
    rewarding, 192–193

in technology investment modeling, 148
systems analysis, 174–181
systems applications, 79
systems measurements, 181–183

T

Tales from the Crypt, **Data Communications** magazine, 86–89
team
  See project team
team development, 41–44
technology investment modeling
  See also computer technology; information technology
  cost savings, 128–138
  profit increase, 132, 138–145
  quantitative model, 156–159
  quick payback on, 126–127
  return on investment (ROI), 118, 156
  risks, 143–145
  success factors, 148
  as a tracking device, 127–128, 156
technology risks, 143–145
time factor, in project management, 48, 50–51
Toles Company, 38
traffic statistics, 180
training, computer technology, 120–121
trend analysis, 179

U

University of Texas at Austin, xiii, 187
university-wide information systems, 196
U.S. Forest Service, 187
user ownership, 52
utility-type computer groups, 119–120, 123

V

value, 78
versioning, applications software, 50
virtual corporations, 38–39, 215
viruses, 5

W

WalMart, 30
WAN (Wide Area Network), 87–89
Wilson, Wm. B., 124
work flow, 58–60, 61–62, 69, 95
World Wide Web (WWW)
  advantages, 44
  Homepage technology, 138–140
  revolution, 39–40

Y

Yale University, xiii

Z

zero-base budgeting, 149
zero-defect information system, 4

PROPERTY OF
TRANS UNION